Praise for *Here Comes the Sun*

"My daughter Michelle was seventeen years old when she died of leukemia after a ten-month battle with the disease. Through it all she never questioned 'why me?' We failed to find a match for Michelle, yet her dying wish to me was to keep up the search so that others could benefit from our efforts to 'find the match.' *Here Comes the Sun*, written by Brian Lucas, is an inspirational story about his wife, Betsy, and the trials and tribulations their family endured during her battle with cancer. It is a book filled with tears and ultimately smiles, for today Betsy is cured.

Somewhere up above Michelle Carew is happy."

—Rod Carew, Baseball Hall of Fame, Cooperstown, NY

"*Here Comes The Sun* is not just a story of one family's cancer journey, it is also a celebration of the strength of community. From the extraordinary caregivers and researchers at the University of Minnesota, to the selfless gift of a young man in Germany, Brian Lucas' remarkable story highlights the importance of reaching out to others, and shows what we can accomplish together."

—Walter Mondale, former vice president of the United States

"Intensely personal, heartrending, and terrifying. What happened to this family could happen to any of us, and yet with wisdom and love, Brian Lucas shows us how a path was found through the fear and pain. Inspiring."

—Arthur Phillips, author of *Prague*, *The Egyptologist*, *Angelica*, *The Song Is You*, and *The Tragedy of Arthur*

"*Here Comes the Sun* kept me on edge. With complications seeming to crop up just when things were starting to look good, the book took me on a life-shaking emotional roller-coaster. Brian Lucas has written a beautiful story. The strength and determination shown by Brian and Betsy, by their daughters and Betsy's mother, by their donor, and by all of the medical personnel involved has to be an inspiration to others going through this now."

—Barbara Delinsky, *New York Times* best-selling author of Sweet Salt Air

"A heartfelt journey of family, love, ups and downs, and the shock of realities we face. *Here Comes The Sun* is a testament to the progress and limitations of medicine. Most importantly, it provides a vision of hope and togetherness and the value of teams at all levels (family, friend, support, medical). This is why I love my job."

—Dr. Jeffrey Miller, hematologist/oncologist, Masonic Cancer Center, University of Minnesota

"This book is for all of us. Each of us has a crucible moment, when we make a choice to believe, to dig deep into our own resources, to open ourselves to the loving care and support of others and to act with courage. Each of us can find inspiration in this story, for whichever role we are called upon to play: spouse or partner, parent, neighbor, friend, professional. Only together can we grow through life's darkest moments, emerging again into the light. Thank you, Brian and Betsy, for this important gift."

—Marilyn Carlson Nelson, retired CEO, Carlson, author of *How We Lead Matters*

"*Here Comes The Sun* shows that by bringing together people with love and support, especially during times of need, great and miraculous things can happen. Thanks to Brian Lucas' powerful sharing of his family's journey, this book will bring even more people together."

—Sona Mehring, founder and CEO of CaringBridge

"*Here Comes The Sun* candidly retells a young family's daunting journey through the dark clouds of illness into the bright sunshine of hope, healing, and thanksgiving. As a clergyman, I have spent many hours with families who have wandered the wilderness of uncertainty and fear that is sickness. Brian Lucas offers both a practical and a spiritual roadmap through that wilderness. *Here Comes The Sun* is not only for families fighting cancer. It is for all of us who might grow in our appreciation of the blessings of family and friends, love and life…and that is all of us."

—Rabbi Joshua M. Davidson, senior rabbi, Congregation Emanu-El of the City of New York

"At a time when experts are asking if our nation's children (not to mention their parents) have the grit it takes to withstand life's ups and downs, Brian Lucas brings us the ultimate handbook of resilience. The Lucas family journey—guided not only by their bravery, but also the tireless work of the medical community and one very compassionate teenager—will give you hope that when it matters most, we can face our most crushing challenges with courage, humor, and love."

—Elizabeth Foy Larsen, co-author of *Unbored: The Essential Field Guide to Serious Fun*

"The remarkable honesty and poignant detail contained in this story will resonate with anyone who has walked with a loved one through a devastating diagnosis and brutal treatment course. There is such hope and comfort in the descriptions of life's simple pleasures inexplicably found in the most unwelcome circumstances.

Nurses will recognize the miracle of seeing patients and families find unbelievable strength and resiliency while navigating life's most difficult and painful moments. The opportunity to so closely observe these triumphs of body and spirit are the heart of nursing and inspire our most gentle and best care.

Brian Lucas' story speaks to our shared experience as human beings as it illuminates how the ties that bind us to one another nurture hope, courage, and healing. It is a beautiful story."

—Sara Froyen Gernbacher, RN, CPHON, nurse case manager, Hematology/Oncology, Children's Hospitals and Clinics of Minnesota

"Raw and powerful in its storytelling, *Here Comes The Sun*, offers an unforgettable journey through the dark night of cancer. Lucas details with brave honesty the point of view of spouse and care-giver, and the result is a profoundly inspiring love story.

This book is of immeasurable value to anyone facing that moment when everything changes. In other words, all of us."

—Annie Sundberg, film director, *Knuckleball!, Joan Rivers: A Piece of Work; The Devil Came On Horseback; The Trials of Darryl Hunt*

"A beautiful love story by Brian Lucas, a devoted husband and father who faced the threat of losing his young wife Betsy to leukemia. The perils associated with her bone marrow transplant, and the courageous way she responded, was very personal for me. The book evokes memories of the heartwrenching challenges that we faced as my wife Barb went with a bone marrow transplant to overcome multiple myeloma."

—Steve Wilkinson, founder of Tennis and Life Camps and a stage IV kidney cancer survivor

"Brian Lucas, with his wife's help, has superbly chronicled the BMT journey from his own perspective as the spouse of a leukemia survivor who also survived just about every complication and attendant procedure of BMT. This story will be of great value to those facing the two steps forward and one step back of a bone marrow transplant, and the importance of fathers learning how to do pigtails and French braids."

—Dr. Bruce Bostrom, Hematology/Oncology, Children's Hospitals and Clinics of Minnesota

"*Here Comes the Sun* is a poignant, descriptive, personal telling of one family's journey through cancer. This compelling, masterfully written book underscores the unique nature of each cancer journey, while giving the reader insight into the roller-coaster of questions, emotions and challenges faced by everyone swept into the wake of a cancer diagnosis."

—Ruth Bachman, author of *Growing Through the Narrow Spots*

"Brian Lucas' description of his family's journey is an eloquent, albeit painful, portrayal of the harsh realities of bone marrow transplantation. As a pediatric oncologist, I witness the ups and downs of everyday life that Brian and Betsy have endured. But I have never experienced it through a family member's eyes. For that I am grateful. Reading this account has touched my life and my career."

—Dr. Joanna Perkins, Hematology/Oncology, Children's Hospitals and Clinics of Minnesota

"The physical and emotional toll on patients and their families during a transplant is difficult to understand unless one has lived through it. Brian Lucas takes us there in *Here Comes The Sun*, a personal diary detailing the inner strength and will to survive of his wife, Betsy, the resiliency of the human spirit, and ultimately their triumph over cancer."

—Dr. Linda Burns, hematologist/oncologist, Masonic Cancer Center, University of Minnesota

"*Here Comes The Sun* is a moving story about the power of both medicine and spirit in the fight against cancer. Brian Lucas describes his family's emotional journey through a fight with blood cancer. While science has made great strides, much work remains. As a cancer researcher, Betsy's story drives me to work even harder to find solutions to these devastating diseases."

—Peter Espenshade, PhD, Professor of Cell Biology,
Johns Hopkins University School of Medicine

Here Comes the Sun

· ·

A Young Family's Journey through Cancer

Here Comes the Sun

A YOUNG FAMILY'S
JOURNEY THROUGH CANCER

BRIAN LUCAS

BEAVER'S POND
PRESS

ISBN: 978-1-59298-975-1
Library of Congress Control Number: 2013912263

Book designed by Mayfly Design and typeset in Adobe Garamond Pro
Cover photograph © Janie Airey/Lifesize/Jupiterimages
Back cover photograph © AleksandarNakic/iStockphoto

Printed in the United States of America
First Printing: 2013

17   16   15   14   13   5   4   3   2   1

Beaver's Pond Press, Inc.
7108 Ohms Lane
Edina, MN 55439-2129
(952) 829-8818
www.BeaversPondPress.com

To order, visit www.BeaversPondBooks.com
or call (800) 901-3480. Reseller discounts available.

www.BrianLucasAuthor.com

To Betsy, Julia, and Molly—

For demonstrating the true power of love and for helping me always keep perspective on what is really important.

Phyllis,

Thanks for your interest in our journey.

All the best,

[signature]

9/23/13

Contents

Acknowledgements

Every aspect of this book has been a team effort. First and foremost, I am grateful to Betsy for her strength, bravery, and the beauty she brings to my life, and to Julia and Molly for making us happy every single day.

Thanks to our family: To Susan for demonstrating the depth of a mother's love. To Duane for his steady, reassuring nature. To John for his positive spirit. To my parents for their unending love and support. And to Jane and Jim, Mark and Amy, Caroline and Basil, and to Malissa for always being there for us.

Thanks to our new family: To Tobias for giving Betsy a new chance at life. To Marleen for making us feel like part of the family. And to our extended family in Germany who welcomed us with open arms and kind hearts.

Thanks to our medical family: Dr. Morrison and Dr. Flint. To Dr. Miller and the rest of the BMT docs at the University of Minnesota who perform miracles every day. To Tanya. To Kelly and to all the other incredible nurses who cared for Betsy. We felt safe in your care, and we appreciated your ability to walk us down that narrow path to a cure.

Thank you to Todd, Bonnie, and Emily for being heroes to us. We will never forget the gifts you gave to those around you, and we will keep you in our hearts forever. Also thank you to all the others who have shared their stories with us and fought bravely. We remain inspired by you all.

Thank you to Dr. John Kersey, a close family friend and a pioneer in the area of bone marrow transplantation at the University of Minnesota. Dr. Kersey died unexpectedly in March 2013. Betsy's life is a testament to the legacy of work Dr. Kersey leaves behind.

Thank you to all the folks at Beaver's Pond Press who helped get this book polished and ready for the world.

Finally, thank you to Team Betsy, the massive support system that sprouted across the country and overseas, supplying us with thoughts, prayers, and support that helped pull us through. Your role in this story is immeasurable.

Introduction

There have been many moments in my life that have prompted me to pause, look around, and wonder, "How on earth did I end up here?"

It happened in college when I was working on a radio show and had the chance to interview Tom Brokaw in his office at Rockefeller Center.

It happened the first time I went on the air as a radio reporter, trying to get through a live report without running out of oxygen and passing out.

When I was a television reporter in La Crosse, Wisconsin and I found myself suiting up with the fire department and going into a "live burn," it happened again.

And when I watched my wife walk down the aisle toward me in her wedding dress, I gave thanks for all the moments that somehow led me to that particular place, at that particular time.

But none of these memories, and none of those moments, compares to the day when I stood in a room at the Blood and Marrow Transplant Clinic (BMT) at the University of Minnesota, six years after our wedding day, listening to a doctor break down the chances of my wife surviving cancer.

This book is the story of the path we took through cancer, and how a combination of science, serendipty, strength, and love helped us face a challenge that we didn't ask for and had no choice but to accept.

Much like that first live report on the radio, at times this fight took my breath away. Similar to when I walked into a burning building, there were moments when I was overcome with fear but had no choice but to keep moving forward. And throughout the journey, I had moments of awe and wonder watching my wife move down a different path, a winding road, that again led toward a future we could share together.

This book is not just about cancer. At its heart, this is a love story. It was love for each other and for our daughters, and love from those around us, that kept us going. And it is this love that continues to help us every day, through a story that is far from over, but has already taken us to places we never imagined we would go.

CHAPTER 1

· · · · · · · · · · · ·

In the Blink of an Eye

The clichés talk about how life can turn "in a heartbeat," or "at the drop of a dime," but in my case life changed between the ring of my cell phone and the appearance of a number on caller ID.

I knew Betsy was at the doctor that morning, and I could tell she was concerned about the sudden rash and swelling that had developed in her leg. Somehow, as soon as I saw that she was calling my cell phone to track me down, I knew something was wrong.

"I need you to come to the doctor's office."

That was all she said.

Her voice said a lot more.

She was calm, direct, using as few words as possible. She was trying to hold things together.

"What's going on? What are they telling you?" I needed something more. A hint of what she knew.

"They're going to run some tests. I need you here."

"I'm heading to the car . . . I'll be there soon."

I left my meeting without an explanation. I drove to the doctor's office. My head was already spinning with questions.

Part of me had known something was wrong. All weekend, as Betsy lay in bed with her leg elevated, I believe we both knew on some level that it was serious. We were on edge. We were a little irritable with each other. We read the information they gave us about possible causes of leg swelling. When we saw the word "cancer," we tried to breeze past the word, or discount it, but I know we both thought about the possi-

1

bility. Maybe it was because a good family friend had just passed away from cancer, or maybe it was because we knew.

I walked into the doctor's office, not sure I was in the right place, and a receptionist called out to me asking if I was Betsy's husband. I said, "Yes." She asked me to follow her back to a room. That kind of urgency is never a good sign. My heart pounded as I opened the door and saw Betsy sitting in a chair. When I saw her tears, I felt a pit in my stomach.

I sat next to her and took her hand. She explained what was going on.

My first thought was how strong her voice was. She was obviously upset but she was pulling it together to fill me in. This was the first of countless times during this fight that she would amaze me.

By this time, I knew it had to be cancer. I was waiting to hear what kind.

"They're pretty sure I have leukemia."

My first thought was, "Leukemia...okay...I think that's curable." When I was in high school, one of my classmates died from leukemia, but I was sure I had read about great progress in fighting the disease over the years. Part of me was actually relieved...for a moment.

The doctor came in and started giving us more information. We were being sent directly to a hospital for further testing to determine what type of leukemia we were dealing with (there are multiple kinds?) and how advanced the cancer was. (She had had no other symptoms. We have to be catching it early, right?)

The doctor was amazing. Compassionate. Smart. She was also a young mother and I got the sense that she felt a great deal of empathy toward Betsy. She took the time to answer all our questions and we never felt like she was trying to wrap things up so she could get to her next patient. She cried with us. She impressed me.

Betsy and I drove to the hospital together. We alternated between silence—both of our heads swimming with thoughts and fears—and talk that already had an element of fight in its tone. Betsy squeezed my hand. "We're going to beat this." I really had no idea what "this" was, but I believed her.

At the hospital another doctor explained more about what we knew. This is when I first heard the term CML and learned about the various forms of leukemia. Betsy was diagnosed with chronic myelogenous leukemia (CML), a relatively rare type of leukemia, but also one that has seen miraculous advances in recent years, with new drugs offering very effective treatment.

This is also the first time I heard about the possibility of a bone marrow transplant. I had no real idea what that entailed other than that it offered hope for a cure.

Again, this doctor stayed with us until we had no more questions. She asked us about our family, our daughters. She looked at the pictures Betsy carries with her. She cried with us as well. I found the tears comforting in some way. I felt like compassionate people were caring for Betsy—people who understood how important it was for her to get better.

A third doctor, the oncologist, shed more light on the tests that Betsy would receive and said we would determine a course of treatment in a couple of days. Betsy would have to stay in the hospital until then.

And just like that—one phone call, two car rides, and three meetings with doctors later—our lives changed forever. We went from husband and wife and father and mother to cancer patient and caregiver in the blink of an eye... or in the ring of a cell phone.

One of the first things we had to do as we waited for Betsy's room to be ready was to call our families. I had a variety of emotions making these calls. First, I dreaded breaking the news. Second, I feared actually uttering the word "cancer," almost as if saying it out loud would officially make this bad dream a reality. Third, and most important, Betsy and I both wanted to get word out quickly—to get more brains working, to get help dealing with the realities of how this would change our lives, and to get our families on board for the fight.

The phone calls went by in a blur. I could only hear one side of Betsy's conversation with her stepfather, whom she reached first, and then her mom, but even just hearing Betsy's side of the conversation I could tell they were incredibly strong from the start. I thought about Betsy's mom hearing this news and assumed she would break down. She didn't. She said, "We're getting on a flight and will be there later today." She flew from Chicago to Minneapolis that day not having any idea she would be staying for more than a year.

The other calls went much the same way—Betsy's father and sister, my mom and dad, my brother. Everyone was shocked, concerned, and had lots of questions, but most of all they were determined to help us through this.

Each of our family members started informing others in our circle: Betsy's stepsisters, our extended family, and close family friends. This experience taught us about the importance of having a large team behind you, and the ranks of Betsy's team grew quickly. Prayers, thoughts, wishes, advice—all of it started flowing immediately. It's easy to get cynical about society these days, but the truth is that there are a lot of good people in the world, and the way people come together in times of need is inspiring.

CHAPTER 2

. . . .

A Storybook Beginning

Betsy was thirty-four years old when she was diagnosed. We had been married for six years.

We were set up on a blind date when I moved back to Minneapolis in 1997. My mom's business partner, Linda, is an old friend of Betsy's family, and when she heard I was moving back to town she set us up.

Our first meeting was a truly blind date. I had never met Betsy before, and had no idea what to expect when I showed up at her apartment. The only information I had to go on was from a brief phone call setting up the meeting time and place.

I arrived for our first date about twenty minutes early because I wasn't sure where her apartment was. I didn't want to wait in my car in front of her building in case she happened to walk by and see me sitting there, so I drove a few blocks away to wait, listening to music and trying not to get too nervous.

When the time came, I drove back to her building and dialed her apartment from the lobby phone. She picked up and said she'd be right down. I waited for what seemed like an eternity. At one point a woman about our age walked past me into the apartment, and I was sure it must be a friend of Betsy's assigned to walk past and give her a report on me before she came down. (Betsy denies this, but I still have my suspicions.)

Finally, Betsy opened the door and walked into the entryway. My first thought was a big "Thank you!" to Linda. Betsy looked beautiful, and her bright smile immediately calmed my nerves.

We walked to our date. I had tickets to an event at the Guthrie Theater celebrating the career of Jessica Lange. It was nice to be able to walk and talk.

I learned that Betsy was a kindergarten teacher working at a Spanish immersion school in Minneapolis. She had lived in Spain and was fluent in Spanish. I could sense her passion for her job and her love of teaching. The more I heard, the more impressed I became.

By the time our evening was over, I was intrigued. I asked her on a second date before dropping her off from that first one. Five months later I was ring shopping. And nine months after we first met, I asked her to marry me at the top of a mountain in Montana.

Our engagement was a simple case of, "When you know, you know." It was easy. It seemed natural. It's hard to describe, but when I was with her, it simply felt as if that was where I belonged.

When we called Linda to tell her we were engaged, we asked her if she was surprised that her "set up" had worked out so well. She said she wasn't surprised at all, that was why she had set us up in the first place.

Betsy is someone who is easy to get to know. In fact, when you are with her, it often feels like she knows everyone. We both grew up in Minneapolis, and our families know a lot of the same people. She was a good friend to the sister of one of my friends growing up. I remember being at his house and always seeing a pack of girls running around. It turns out Betsy was one of the girls in that pack.

Betsy went to a lot of different schools growing up, and she maintains friendships with people from every class. No matter where we go—around Minneapolis, or anywhere in the country—it seems like Betsy always runs into people she knows. She takes an interest in everyone she meets and makes quick and deep connections.

I remember going through some of the e-mails that Betsy received when she was diagnosed, and asking her about one of the names I didn't recognize. She said, "Oh, she's a mom that I met standing in line to sign up for a class a few months ago." From the sound of the e-mail, I thought this woman was one of Betsy's oldest friends. Betsy's ability to connect and her vast network of friends proved to be a great source of strength through her fight. I could relate to why people are drawn to her, and I was thankful for all the people who came forward to express their love for Betsy in her time of need.

From that first date, through our wedding and the births of our daughters, I had always felt like we were living a storybook life. And even when that story took a sudden and unexpected turn, I was always able to look back on that first date, when Betsy came out of her apartment and smiled at me, as the moment when life came into focus, and an amazing journey began.

CHAPTER 3

. . . .

The Strength of Children

The shock of a cancer diagnosis immediately knocks you on your heels, and that was definitely the case for us. But fear and uncertainty quickly gave way to determination, and I'm convinced that we were able to get refocused quickly for one reason: our daughters.

When Betsy was diagnosed, Julia was three and Molly was ten months old. They are incredible girls.

People often ask me how Betsy and I managed to keep things together through all we've been through with two children to care for. My response is always the same. I can't imagine how we could have made it through *without* them.

No matter what I was dealing with every day—during the diagnosis, transplant, and recovery—I could always count on one bright moment: seeing the girls. The day of Betsy's diagnosis, when I went home, they effortlessly accomplished what I thought would be impossible. They made me smile.

The same thing happened when we brought Julia and Molly to the hospital for the first time. I was worried that seeing them would make Betsy break down, but they bounded into the room, Julia crawled onto Betsy's bed and started playing with the controls, and the mood of the room lifted.

Julia and Molly were in very different places in terms of dealing with Betsy's illness. At ten months, Molly was obviously too young to know that anything was going on. We were lucky to be able to call upon Betsy's mom, Susan, to take over a great deal of the caregiving, so Molly continued to get all the attention she was used to receiving.

Molly was born about a month premature, and she had to spend a week in a special care nursery before she could come home. Like her mom, she was a fighter from the beginning.

I remember following the nurses as they whisked Molly from the delivery room into a separate area where they check the vital signs of premature babies. I nervously peeked over their shoulders, praying that this tiny, tiny baby was doing okay. I was relieved when the nurses started to laugh. Molly was squirming around with so much vigor that one of the nurses turned to me with a smile and said, "You've got a feisty daughter here. She's going to be fine."

Despite her rough start, it seemed like Molly was smiling from the moment she was born. Even before babies are supposed to be able to really "smile," her expressions conveyed so much joy—her mouth, her cheeks, and her sparkling eyes convinced me that her smiles were the real thing and not, as they say, "just gas."

The older she grew, the wider that smile became. And ten months after her birth, as her mom faced the fight of her life, Molly's smile continued to be a beacon for us, bringing us out of our heads and back into the moment.

The only real impact leukemia had on Molly at that young age was a change in her primary caregivers, a change that was harder on Betsy than Molly.

Betsy's mom assumed Betsy's day-to-day role, and I tried to get as much quality time with Molly and Julia as I could. Molly formed a deep attachment to Susan, and even during times when Betsy's role was able to expand into more day-to-day parenting, Molly would call out to me in the middle of the night, or would go to Susan if she fell and hurt herself.

It only made things worse when Molly was sick. Betsy wasn't able to go near the girls if they weren't feeling well for fear of infection, so in Molly and Julia's most needy moments, Betsy had to keep her distance.

I remember one time in particular I was reading to Molly and giving her a bottle before bed. Susan had taken a rare night off to go out with some friends. Out of nowhere, Molly started throwing up—a lot—and I got drenched. I yelled out in surprise and Betsy came upstairs to see what was going on. I told her to stay out of the room and asked her to just throw me some towels.

While it might seem like a nice reprieve to not have to help clean up after a mess like that, I know it was really hard for Betsy to be reduced to an observer of that scene. Mopping up that mess would have been a small price to pay to be able to comfort her baby. And to be honest, I would have welcomed her help as well.

I knew it would just be a matter of time before Betsy would reassume her rightful place as a primary caregiver for Molly. Still, I cringed every time Molly came to me or to Susan instead of Betsy, and I remember feeling such relief the first time I heard Molly call out for "Mama" when she was distressed. I may have imagined it, but I believe the ensuing hug from Betsy had a little extra strength as well.

While cancer didn't really mean anything to Molly, it was a different story for Julia.

From the very beginning, Julia seemed to have an understanding of the situation that was well beyond her years. In fact, before Betsy was diagnosed, Julia already had a curiosity about blood and diseases that belied her age.

About a month before the diagnosis, Julia was looking through a bookshelf and happened to pull out a book that Betsy used when she taught kindergarten. The book is called *A Drop of Blood,* and it lays out all the basics about blood and the role the cells play in the human body.

Julia wanted us to read that book to her at bedtime. It became the book of choice every night for weeks.

After the diagnosis, we were careful to not share too much with Julia right away. But in those first days, when we sat down with her to explain what was going on, it helped that Julia was already well versed about red blood cells, white blood cells and platelets.

Betsy explained that her "blood was sick" and that her body was "making too many white blood cells."

Julia nodded quietly.

"So I'm going to the doctor to get cured. It's going to take a lot of work, but Mommy's going to be fine."

Julia gave Betsy a hug.

I know Julia didn't grasp the bigger picture or have any idea what the implications of this fight were, but I got the feeling she understood on a basic level, and was determined to help her mommy through a difficult time.

Julia took on an important role in the fight. At various times she was Betsy's cheerleader, comic relief, snuggler, and sympathizer.

It wasn't always easy for her. Like Molly, she had to accept the fact that Betsy wasn't around for long stretches of time and often couldn't be there for her, even when she was home. But most of the time, Julia had an amazing amount of perspective.

I remember watching her eat lunch with a friend when he suddenly looked at her and said, "So your mom has cancer?"

My heart pounded as I waited to see how Julia would react. Julia simply looked up from her sandwich and said, "Yeah..." and went back to eating. There was no sense of shame, hurt, or sadness. It was a remarkably matter-of-fact exchange between three-year-olds. I was so proud of her.

Another time, Julia came home from school and told us about an exchange that she had had with a classmate that day. A friend of hers approached her and said, "Your mom has cancer?"

Julia said, "Yes."

The girl said, "So...she's going to die."

It wasn't a question. It was stated like a fact.

When Julia told Betsy this story, Betsy took Julia in her arms and said, "You know what, Julia? That girl doesn't know your mommy."

That was good enough for Julia.

We tried hard to maintain a positive outlook for Julia even in the most difficult times. At bedtime I would often ask her if there was anything on her mind or any questions she had about what was going on with Momma. Often she said she didn't have any questions, but sometimes she did.

"Why does Mommy have to stay in her hospital room all the time?"

"Does it hurt when they take the blood from Mommy's port?"

"How did Mommy get cancer?"

It made me feel good to know that Julia felt comfortable talking about the situation and asking questions. I would do my best to answer, but sometimes I had to admit I just didn't know the answer. Even that was good enough for her. I think it was more important for her just to ask.

While we always tried to be honest, we also made a point to maintain our optimism that Betsy was going to be fine.

The remarkable thing was that during some particularly scary times, Julia would impart this sense of optimism right back to us. She never failed to give an extra hug and kiss when they were most needed, both to me and to Betsy. I'll never understand how she could be so perceptive and strong at such a young age.

Leukemia is a terrible disease. CML is rare. There is no known cause, and the chances of Betsy getting this diagnosis were incredibly remote. We have had numerous moments of anger and frustration. But not once have we lost sight of a simple truth: We are lucky. We have two beautiful daughters. We have each other. We have incredible and supportive families. And as formidable a foe as cancer is, it can't take that away from us.

Illness teaches you a lot. There are so many things that we didn't know we should be thankful for before this fight that we now appreciate. We always appreciated our girls. We just didn't know how much strength we would draw from them at such a young age.

CHAPTER 4

. . . .

Reality Sets In

Betsy, Julia, and Molly are the center of my world. And in a moment, that world was knocked off of its orbit. All due to that simple word: leukemia.

After the whirlwind of that first day, the initial diagnosis, further tests, informing our families, and sorting through this new reality in our own minds, I left Betsy at the hospital and headed home to get some sleep.

When I stepped in the door, it was like stepping into an alternate universe. I was entering our house, but suddenly it didn't feel like home.

My head was spinning as I walked in. Susan and Duane, Betsy's stepfather, were already there getting settled in. Julia and Molly were asleep.

I gave a brief update about how Betsy was doing and the plan for the following day. Susan and Duane asked a few questions. I gave a few answers. We talked and listened and processed, but we didn't really connect. I noticed the faraway expression in Susan's eyes, and I was sure I wore the same expression.

None of us quite knew what to say, how to feel, or what to do. We were feeling our way through this situation, trying to process it. We wanted to be there for each other but we weren't really there ourselves.

I decided to take our dog, Bella, for a walk. It was dark, probably close to midnight. Bella and I walked slowly down the street and back. I sat down with her in our backyard and stared up at the sky. I may have looked like I was lost in my thoughts, but the truth is I didn't know what to think. I churned over the events of the day. I cried. My stomach hurt. And I kept looking up into the sky trying to make sense of things.

Then I went back in the house, got ready for bed, kissed Molly in her crib and Julia in her bed, and tried to sleep.

I have no idea how long it took to fall asleep. It felt like a long time but I didn't look at the clock. All I know is that eventually it was morning. I made it to day two of the journey. That was a start.

When I saw Betsy at the hospital the morning after her diagnosis I broke down crying. She cried. We took turns being strong and sad. I was glad that we never both hit sad at the same time. We needed each other.

One of the first orders of business that first day in the hospital was to get a feel for what was really happening with Betsy's bone marrow. That meant a bone marrow biopsy.

When I first heard the term "bone marrow biopsy" I assumed this was a blood test. When they wheeled a procedure cart into the room I immediately realized this was going to be a little more involved.

The last time I had seen a cart rolled into a room like that was when Molly was born, and they came in to give Betsy her epidural.

I soon learned that getting a sample of bone marrow is a similarly discomforting procedure. Bone marrow resides in the interior of bones. In adults, the primary locations for active bone marrow production are the hipbone and the sternum. For bone marrow biopsies, the hipbone is the location of choice for harvesting cells.

The woman who did the biopsy was very good about talking Betsy through the procedure. She explained everything she was doing and said she would warn Betsy when the difficult parts were coming. From my vantage point, holding Betsy's hand, I had a clear view of what was going on. If I had been watching the procedure being performed on a stranger it would have been cringeworthy. Watching it being done to my wife was heartbreaking.

They gave Betsy some IV pain medication and had her lie on her stomach. They then started pressing on her hipbones to try to find a good flat spot where they could get some "leverage." When they found a good spot, they marked it with a pen.

Betsy squeezed my hand as they started to give her a local anesthetic, putting the needle into her hip over and over to get a good area of coverage. They then started to numb the bone, applying the anesthetic while tapping the bone with the needle. I was surprised by how loud the tapping was on the bone. I tried not to let that surprise come out in my voice as I reassured Betsy that everything was going to be all right.

When Betsy confirmed that she could no longer feel the tapping on her bone, they began the extraction.

They started by twisting a large needle into her bone. The needle had a handle like a corkscrew, to let the physician's assistant (PA) get a good grip and apply strong pressure to get through the bone. She twisted the needle slowly, applying constant pressure to the bone, until she could feel that she was through. She then flipped a switch on the handle to capture the bone fragment that she had just cored out of the hip. She extracted a small sliver of bone and placed it in a jar for the lab.

I thought the bone extraction marked the end of the procedure, but it was only the end of part one. They had to go back into the bone, in a different spot, to get the marrow samples.

So once again, the PA pushed and twisted the needle into Betsy's hip. It was hard work, and she had to stop and rest a couple of times with the needle still stuck in the bone.

This time, when she made it all the way into the bone cavity, she attached a large syringe to the needle. She told Betsy to take a deep breath and warned her, "You're going to feel this all the way down to your toes."

She then pulled on the syringe to start extracting the marrow. Betsy gasped and squeezed my hand to the point where I was worried my bones were going to audibly crack. I watched the syringe fill with a few ounces of cloudy red fluid. It was marrow, mixed with blood. And they were getting a good sample.

The PA unscrewed the syringe and handed the sample to her assistant. She then attached another empty syringe and made another draw. More gasping. I was better prepared this time for the hard squeeze of my hand. I think in anticipation I actually squeezed back.

Then it was over. The PA told Betsy everything went well and they got good samples. They took out the needle and put gauze over the hole in her hip, which was flowing with blood. Betsy was a model patient, even thanking the PA when it was over for doing a great job. I had to smile. Not many people would say "thank you" to someone who had just put them through that much pain. This was the first of many biopsies that Betsy would endure. She said "thank you" every single time.

A few hours after the biopsy we had a meeting with our oncologist and I started to feel a little better. I could tell we were in good hands.

Betsy is a fighter. And sitting in her room, holding her hand, gave me more and more reassurance that she had the strength and resolve to beat this. It was only when I went home that night that I started to feel scared again.

I couldn't sleep, so I typed. I wanted to get word out to Betsy's friends about the diagnosis.

· · · · · · · · · · · · · · · · ·

May 25, 2005
Dear friends and family,
    Please forgive this group e-mail, but I felt this was the best way to get information out to you all in a timely manner.
    I'm asking that you all please send your warmest thoughts and

best wishes to Betsy right now as we deal with a health issue that has caught us all by surprise.

Last Thursday, Betsy started to feel some itching on her right shin and her leg appeared swollen. On Friday, she went to the doctor where they drew blood and prescribed an antibiotic on the theory that she had some sort of infection. The doctor advised her to return on Monday if things hadn't improved. Betsy spent the weekend with her leg elevated, but the antibiotics didn't seem to be helping, so she followed the doctor's advice and returned Monday morning.

Immediately upon arrival, Betsy could tell that the doctor was concerned. Betsy's white cell count had been elevated on Friday, so the doctor had, thankfully, been proactive and sent the blood to be analyzed. A second blood test showed a much higher white cell count and some abnormal cells. The suspicion quickly turned to leukemia.

Betsy called me at work and I came to the clinic where we spoke with the doctor some more. Arrangements were already made for us to check into a hospital for testing. We left immediately for the hospital where Betsy has undergone a series of procedures including a bone marrow biopsy, a difficult procedure that is only made bearable by the promise that it will yield specific answers about her condition.

The bottom line at this time is this: We are almost positive that Betsy has chronic myelogenous leukemia (CML). This is a cancer that results in the production of too many white blood cells. We will get more details tomorrow and will begin to determine a course of treatment. All indications are that we are catching this early…and there have been terrific strides made around CML in recent years. Still, as you can imagine, we are dealing with a great deal of fear, sadness, and uncertainty.

I can't even begin to describe the shock of the last two days…and the feelings of helplessness. Betsy is truly a remarkable woman. She has been strong and determined to get to the bottom of this. At the same time she has been so warm and caring to those around her. I am inspired by her and in awe of her.

Betsy's family has stepped in to take care of Julia and Molly while I've been at the hospital. Both of our families have been the source of incredible support and strength. The girls visited Betsy in the hospital today and brought an immediate dose of joy to the room. They are such wonderful girls. It says a lot that, despite the news of the last two days, Betsy and I still can look at each other and comment about how truly lucky we are—we have two amazing daughters, incredible families, and wonderful friends like you.

As we get set to plan our treatment, we need your help. I am a firm believer that positive thoughts and prayers can have a profound impact. We ask you to please send as much as you have to Betsy in the coming days.

I will try to send updates as I have them. In the meantime, please send your best wishes. We need all the help we can get.

Thank you,

Brian

. . . .

I sent out the message to every e-mail address I could find. It went out around 1:30 in the morning. For some reason, simply typing the words made me feel better. And when I sent the e-mail, even though I was sure it was too late for anyone to read it, I immediately felt stronger, like the cavalry would soon be on its way to help drive the bandits out of town.

I went to see Betsy early the next morning. When I came home to tuck the girls into bed, I checked my e-mail. I watched the inbox numbers start to change...twenty e-mails...forty e-mails...eighty e-mails...one hundred e-mails...when my inbox stopped loading it showed 115 e-mails in less than one day.

I started to read them.

. . . .

"Brian, I just read your e-mail. Oh my God. We are so worried about Betsy. What hospital is she staying in?

I know your in-laws are here, but please know that you can bring the kids by anytime, or I can bring my guys over and watch them so you can be at the hospital or appointments as you need to. Anytime."

"I love you. I'm praying for you. As I sit crying in my office at the news, I can't even imagine how devastating it is for you. We want to help in any way we can."

"Every single ounce of positive energy that my body can muster is going to you all. I will do everything I can from a distance—and when you're ready you can call on me for absolutely anything. Child-care, quick visits, long visits, cleaning, laundry, Bella-care, bad jokes, whatever. You will be at the front of my mind today, tomorrow, the next day, and on and on. I am always here for you."

"Words cannot describe my sadness that your minds, hearts and emotions have had to go down this path. I literally have been unable to think about anything else but Betsy since I heard the news. Please know that we are praying for you and will continue to do so."

"I have already placed a call into my great-aunts who are nuns in New York. They have added Betsy to their prayer chain, and believe me, it is very powerful. They got me through my lung cancer twenty years ago.

Please remain strong for her and know that you can count on me and my family for anything."

"My fifteen-year-old niece had a surprise diagnosis of acute lympho-blastic leukemia about two years ago. When they caught it, it was in an advanced stage. Although the odds were against her from the start, her strength and the support of family and friends (and, of course, wonderful doctors and treatment) pulled her through a very tough time and she is in complete remission today. The most frightening thing she is dealing with now is getting her driver's license—a wonderfully normal and beautiful thing to see."

"I very much understand the shock, uncertainty, and helplessness you all may be feeling right now because I am also a cancer survivor. Not something I generally talk much about, I don't really know why, but something I'm more than willing to talk about if it's helpful."

"I guess I don't talk about it much, but I believe in prayer, too. And God. And as it happens I read this today before walking out the door to attend a weekly 7:30 a.m. prayer service that I lead at my church over here in St. Paul. It's the Anglican rite of Morning Prayer—it's been said in much the same way for more than four hundred years. Our little group prayed and meditated for you in the quiet of this early morning and we'll do so every week."

Side note: I've always had this thing for cardinals (the birds, that is, not the clerics), and as I left church this morning there was this brilliant red cardinal perched right in front of me, looking my direction, singing his head off. If no one objects, I'm going to take that as a sign that my message today got through."

. . . .

I read through all the messages. I cried.
The cavalry had arrived.

CHAPTER 5

· · · · · · · · · · · · ·

Did You Catch It Early?

As soon as someone is diagnosed with cancer, the same question always comes up: Did you catch it early? There's a fairly universal need to try to get a quick read on how serious it is, and the words "we got it early" can bring at least a small sense of relief.

When Betsy was first diagnosed, "We got it early" was my mantra. Betsy hadn't shown any of the symptoms they were asking us about. Fatigue? No. Weakness? No. Night sweats? No. Fever? No. She'd had plenty of energy and looked healthy. As frightened as I felt when I went home that first night, the one thing I found reassuring was that we had caught it early.

Another more and more universal response to a diagnosis is going on the Internet and researching the illness yourself. The first night I couldn't get myself to Google CML. I was too tired and worried about what I might find. The second night I decided to take a quick look, reminding myself that much of what I would find would probably be unreliable.

At first I was shocked by the number of hits typing "chronic myelogenous leukemia" pulled up on Google. The counter showed more than 800,000 hits. For a disease I had never heard of, there was a lot of information available.

Most of the top links that came up were official sites defining the disease, but certain phrases caught my eye:

- *"Leukemia is a form of cancer unlike any other and one of the more dangerous…"*
- *"Clinical trial: SB-715992 in Treating Patients With Acute Leukemia, Chronic Myelogenous Leukemia, or Advanced Myelodysplastic Syndromes…"*
- *"Support and resources for patients and families of CML patients…"*
- *"Only about 5,000 Americans are diagnosed with CML each year, qualifying it as an 'orphan disease.' About 2,300 die from it annually."*
- *"…survival rate, which is typically about six years in CML."*

Much of what I read was scary. People told stories of long battles with CML. Some patients went into remission; some didn't make it.

The more I read, the more I consoled myself with two thoughts. First, most of the stories took place before a miracle drug called Gleevec had been approved for use with CML. Gleevec had changed the game. It was on the cover of *Time* magazine when it was introduced and was hailed as the first "designer drug" that can attack and kill cancer cells without killing good cells at the same time. As rare as CML is, we were very lucky that Gleevec had been discovered.

The second point I found consoling was that we had "caught it early." There are three stages of CML: chronic, accelerated, and the ominously and appropriately named "blast crisis" phase.

The chronic stage can last for years before it moves to the accelerated phase. There are often no symptoms of chronic stage CML. Cases in this stage are extremely treatable with Gleevec and have a very high recovery rate (around a 90 percent five-year survival rate).

Accelerated patients are starting to see an increase in the "blast cells" in their blood. These are the cells with the defective chromosome that forces the body to produce too many white cells, eventually crowding out the red cells and depriving the body of oxygen and nutrients. Gleevec can still be effective in this phase, but you need to get back to remission quickly before you enter blast crisis, the third and final stage of CML. Patients are determined to be in blast crisis if their percentage of blast cells reaches 20 percent.

Patients in blast crisis have very low survival rates and often only have a matter of months to live. Once the blast cells reach this tipping point the disease gets very aggressive and can be difficult or impossible to bring under control.

When I read these descriptions, I decided that Betsy must be in the chronic stage. I took some comfort knowing that Betsy's blast cell count was low—the first count had shown less than 10 percent. I "diagnosed" Betsy as being in late chronic stage and went to sleep thankful we had "caught it early."

The next morning I called Betsy at the hospital to tell her I was coming in soon. She sounded great, but what she told me took my breath away. She said she had just seen the doctor and had been informed that her blast cells had gone up to 20 percent.

Twenty percent? I could feel my heart pounding in my head. I didn't want to alarm Betsy by telling her about my "research" the night before, but if blast cells had gone from less than 10 percent to 20 percent in one day, we could be looking at blast crisis.

"Did the doctor say anything about starting you on Gleevec?" I asked, in a voice not as calm as I had hoped it would be.

"Yes, we're going to do that. We'll cover that at the meeting today."

"Can you tell him that you'd like to start now?" I implored in the least desperate tone I could muster. "If your blast cells are going up, shouldn't we act sooner than later?"

"They have me started on one drug, but we have to have the meeting to talk about the treatment plan and they want to be sure they have everything diagnosed right before starting Gleevec."

"Okay...I'll be in soon. I love you."

We hadn't caught it early.

· · · · · · · · · · · · · · · · ·

May 27, 2005

Dear friends and family,

I wanted to e-mail an update to let you know what we have learned about Betsy's condition and what steps we are taking now. It would be almost impossible to reply individually to all of you, so I am sending another group message.

First, the best news of all is that Betsy is home! She came home this afternoon after more than three days in the hospital. Having her home and being able to watch her with Julia and Molly again does immeasurable good to my heart. She is an incredible mother, and while the girls were troupers while she was gone, I know how important it is to them and to Betsy to have her home.

As for the illness…we did get final confirmation that she has CML. The bone marrow biopsy left no doubt. When determining what stage you are in with CML they often look to the percentage of "blast cells" you have. These are the cells that are creating the "Philadelphia chromosome" that is the culprit here. Betsy's blast cell percentage is not ideal—it is on the edge of being considered in an acute phase—but the doctors (who have been incredible) have determined that despite this reading, she is not in acute phase and can be treated with Gleevec, a designer drug that produces incredible results for CML patients.

Betsy started on Gleevec yesterday. When she took the first one, we both felt a strange sense of relief—it's so good to have a plan and to get to start this fight. Sitting around and waiting was awful.

We have an appointment next Thursday with a doctor at the University of Minnesota who is renowned for his work with CML and bone marrow transplants. After that we should have a pretty clear view of what's ahead of us, but our best guess is that Betsy will use Gleevec for a few months to get the CML into remission. At that point she will undergo a bone marrow transplant, which will get rid of the CML completely. Betsy's sister is going to be tested as a donor and we're keeping our fingers crossed for a match.

When a loved one is diagnosed with cancer, you have no choice but to learn a lot—quickly. In the past few days I've learned a lot of things that I wish I didn't need to know about. Things like blast cells, Philadelphia chromosomes, chronic vs. acute stages, and a drug called Gleevec that can hopefully work miracles.

At the same time I've also learned (or rather been reminded of) other things. I've seen firsthand how caring, generous, and supportive people can be. Betsy and I have received literally hundreds of e-mails from people across the country. Whether it's a quick note to let us know you're thinking of us, or a story about your own life and experiences related to cancer or other illnesses, each and every e-mail has meant so much to us. I have been printing all of the e-mails so Betsy can read them whenever she needs a lift. Friends have offered help in so many ways. Betsy told me today she feels like there is an army lined up behind her to help her with this fight. You are giving us the strength that we need for this battle, and we really appreciate it.

With the continued support of all of you and countless others, we know we can beat this thing. We are grateful for the tireless help of our families who have stepped in with strength and compassion and helped us in so many ways. And I am particularly thankful for Julia and Molly, who make us smile every time we lay eyes on them, and for Betsy, who throughout this has been a model of grace and resolve to turn this unfortunate circumstance into a footnote to our larger life story. It's amazing…she's the one battling this illness…but she's also been an incredible source of strength to me.

Please keep the positive thoughts and prayers coming. We need the Gleevec to do its job and move this into remission. We have a lot of work left to do, but be sure that your energy is helping us move forward.

Thank you.

Brian, Betsy, Julia, and Molly

· · · · · · · · · · · · · · · · ·

CHAPTER 6

. . . .

Reaching Out

It was clear from the beginning how important it is to reach out to friends and family for support when you're facing a crisis. The e-mail messages we were receiving provided a huge boost to us at a time when we really needed all the positivity we could gather.

We also realized that as soon as you engage people in your battle, you have a responsibility to keep them updated about any developments that occur. Your friends and family are part of the team now, and if you want them to keep sending thoughts, prayers, and positive energy, you need to let them know what's going on.

Initially I relied solely on e-mail to get word out to people. I cobbled together e-mail lists from Betsy's and my address books. I put every name I could find in these lists, figuring it's better to cast a wide net. I then asked people to forward the e-mail to anyone they thought would want to be informed. Many of those people sent me notes asking to be put on the mailing list. The list grew. The team grew.

In the initial batch of responses I received after the first e-mail went out, I had a few people suggest starting a CaringBridge site for Betsy to keep people informed. I had never heard of CaringBridge and wasn't sure how it would help, so I visited the site.

CaringBridge is a nonprofit organization that provides free web pages to families who are dealing with medical issues. You can create a page, add pictures, and post updates on the site so people can check in for new information. There's also a section where people can post messages of support.

It was late at night a few days after the diagnosis when I first browsed the site. I created an account for Betsy and added some pictures. Then I started browsing some of the sample pages. I could see the benefit of the site, but there was something about reading the sample pages and then seeing the page I created with Betsy's picture on it that put a pit in my stomach.

I didn't want to be part of CaringBridge. I didn't want Betsy to have a page. It was almost as though creating that page officially made us part of a community that I didn't want any part of, a community where the price of membership is the diagnosis of a life-threatening disease.

It took me almost a week to open the site again. I was reading e-mails from friends late at night after a particularly tough day and decided to take another look at CaringBridge. It finally struck me that we were part of that community, like it or not, and we were going to need all the help we could get.

I finished creating Betsy's page and sent out an e-mail with the link. I would continue to send e-mails to my mailing lists, but CaringBridge became the main portal of information and messages through our journey. We were astounded by the number of visitors to the page, and lifted up by the beautiful messages from friends and family from literally around the world.

· · · · · · · · · · · · · · · · ·

CaringBridge Update: Friday, June 3, 2005

We had our first meeting with the University of Minnesota doctor today for a full assessment of where we stand and what our course of action should be. The doctor is a very highly regarded expert specializing in CML and bone marrow transplants.

We were feeling optimistic. A blood test earlier in the week showed Betsy's white cell counts going down significantly, so we felt the Gleevec must be working. We were hoping today's meeting would provide confirmation on that and would also help Betsy get relief for the pain and swelling in her ankle which has become almost unbearable and has kept her bedridden ever since she returned home from the hospital.

The anticipation we felt heading into the meeting soon gave way to a stark reality as the doctor ran us through his assessment.

The bottom line is this: We have quite a fight ahead of us.

As I mentioned in my last e-mail, Betsy's blast cell count was hovering around 20 percent. That's higher than we wanted to see and means she's close to being in the acute "blast phase" of CML. While I was aware of that fact, I guess the reality of what that means never really sank in.

Today the doctor laid that out for us. Patients in the blast phase of CML are difficult to treat. Betsy is far enough along in the CML stages that there's a decent chance the Gleevec won't be effective, and we can't afford to wait the six months or so it would take to see whether or not the drug could put her into long-term remission. Betsy needs a bone marrow transplant as soon as possible.

Betsy's sister, Jane, was tested today to see if she is a match for Betsy to be a bone marrow donor. We'll get those results in about ten days. If Betsy and Jane are not a match, we'll move on to the national registry. As soon as we find a match we'll move ahead as quickly as possible toward the transplant. That means intensive chemotherapy and radiation, a transplant, and then six weeks or so of recovery in a sanitary room to prevent infection.

It's an extremely difficult and taxing process, but it is our best hope for a cure.

The only other complicating matter is Betsy's leg and ankle. Nobody has a good sense for why she is in so much pain and what we can do about it. We're going in for a bone scan tomorrow that will hopefully lead to some answers. We need to get this figured out for two reasons: First, she can't have a bone marrow transplant if she's got something wrong with her leg. Second, the pain is debilitating and is preventing her from being able to get out of bed to play with

Molly and Julia, go for walks, and do other things that would give her a great mental boost.

Today was a day that I never imagined I would be part of, but knowing what we're really up against helps us prepare for the fight ahead. Our optimism is due in no small part to all of you, our support system. I continue to print all of the e-mails you send so Betsy can read them. We have been touched by the kindness, love, and generosity that you have shown. We have also been overwhelmed by the cards, flowers, and meals that have been delivered.

This has been a difficult time, but there is so much to be thankful for: We are lucky to have such loving and supporting families. We are lucky to have amazing friends who prop us up. We're so thankful for Molly and Julia who light up the room whenever they are around, and who are a constant reminder of the miracle of life and the boundless capacity of love. And I am especially thankful that I get to be alongside Betsy for this fight. I am amazed by her strength and her compassion for those around her. It was Betsy's words that brought me out of the haze of the meeting this morning. She grabbed my hand and said, "We're going to beat this." I immediately knew it was true. It breaks my heart that my beautiful and caring wife is being forced into this situation. But nobody is more determined than Betsy—and her determination is contagious.

· · · · · · · · · · · · · · · · ·

That first meeting with Betsy's doctor is the closest I have ever come to complete despair. And yet, it was also the moment when I realized just how strong Betsy was, and what a fighter she would prove to be.

Dr. Jeffrey Miller is a nationally renowned physician with the Masonic Cancer Center at the University of Minnesota. He specializes in blood and marrow transplantation and he is doing ground-breaking research into ways to use the body's immune system to fight cancer. We felt good going into our first meeting with him, because there was a general consensus from Betsy's referring doctor and others we spoke to that he was the right person for this case. The care he provided exceeded all our hopes and expectations, but our first meeting proved to be a difficult introduction.

Betsy, her mom, her sister, and I were all crowded into a small clinic room. Betsy was lying on the examination table. We had to wait a while for Dr. Miller to come in. We sat anxiously, waiting to get a clearer picture of Betsy's situation and her odds of recovery.

When Betsy was diagnosed, I read materials that were peppered with percentages. No matter where I looked—"long-term survival"— "five-year survival"—"remission rates"—none of the statistics gave me the kind of reassurance I was looking for. And when I found out Betsy was in blast crisis, the percentages looked worse. Even the "three-month survival rate" started to look startlingly low.

But until our first meeting with Dr. Miller, I had dismissed many of the percentages as not being applicable to Betsy's situation. I wanted to hear from the expert. I was sure he would give us something more positive to grab hold of—a reason why Betsy's prognosis was much better than the numbers I was reading. I was wrong.

Looking at Betsy's blood counts and the progression of her disease, what Dr. Miller told us made my heart hurt.

The chances of curing someone in blast crisis are around 20 percent.

When you start to look at other factors, such as the chance of surviving a bone marrow transplant, the side effects, and the other complications that can occur, you start to get a startlingly bleak picture.

When I heard his assessment of Betsy's situation, my head started to swim. The room got small. For a moment, I felt removed from the situation, like I was floating up above, watching this horrible scene unfold below me. Then, when Betsy grabbed my hand, all of a sudden I was back...in the room...in the moment. And suddenly the numbers, the odds, the percentages took on a different meaning to me.

Dr. Miller explained that he didn't tell us these percentages to scare us, but simply to be sure we understand what we're up against.

"These are just numbers," he said. "Every case is different, and every situation is different."

It's natural, and in many ways it's helpful to use numbers to get a feel for a prognosis. But we finally realized that at the end of the day, the numbers don't mean anything.

First of all, the statistics didn't factor in some very important things that Betsy had going in her favor:

1. She has access to the best health care.
2. She has always been healthy, so she entered her treatment relatively strong.
3. She has lots of support. She can count on her family and friends to help her throughout her treatment and recovery.
4. She has a great attitude and a positive outlook on her recovery.

The other reason you can't take percentages too much to heart is that they are, by definition, just percentages. They are data points based on history.

When you flip a coin, there's always a 50 percent chance it will land on heads. Even if it has landed on heads ten times in a row, the next flip has as much of a chance of landing heads as the last one. Each flip has its own percentage, and history doesn't change that.

So while the odds told one story about Betsy's condition and the expectations for recovery, we saw a different story. The past was not going to dictate how our story would end. And when Betsy grabbed my hand in the clinic on that difficult day, I was suddenly confident our story was just beginning.

CHAPTER 7

· · · · · · · · · · · · ·

Charting Our Path

There was something almost reassuring about getting the straight story about where Betsy was and what she was facing. Now, at least, we could start plotting a course to move forward.

When you're on a journey, the best map in the world doesn't mean a thing if you don't know where you're starting from. After the meeting with Betsy's doctor, we were definitely aware. We were at a place on the map that nobody wants to visit. And the road to a cure was longer and more complicated than we ever thought it would be. But it was a starting point. And now we could focus our energy on making sure each step was directed toward that ultimate goal.

· · · · · · · · · · · · · · · · ·

CaringBridge Update: Wednesday, June 8, 2005

We have learned some more about Betsy's condition and what the implications are for treatment. First, our doctor confirmed that Betsy is definitely in the blast stage of CML. A close examination of her cells shows that another abnormality is showing up beyond the typical Philadelphia chromosome and this is a pretty clear indication of blast crisis CML. This doesn't really change the ultimate course of treatment, but it does make the need for a bone marrow transplant more urgent, and it makes it more likely that the Gleevec won't have the desired effect.

In the coming weeks, we need to find a donor match and get her white cell, blast cell, and platelet counts under control so she can undergo a transplant.

The doctor may add another medication to try to accomplish this, or Betsy may have to undergo some more intense inpatient chemotherapy as soon as next week to try to get everything moving in the right direction.

The other thing we found out is that Betsy's sister is not a match. We are now going to be reaching out to the national registry to find a donor. The good news is that Betsy's marrow doesn't appear to be unusual, so there is strong likelihood for a good match.

Betsy's bone scan came up negative, which is good, but also confusing, since we still don't know why her ankle was in so much pain. The ankle pain has diminished, but Betsy still can't get out of bed due to severe cramping and pain in the muscles of both legs. This may be from the chemotherapy. She can control the pain with medication, but we don't yet know how or when she's going to be able to get up and walk around and play with the girls.

Betsy's mom moved in with us the night we found out about the cancer and has been invaluable for support, help with the girls, and keeping the house in working order. She's been unbelievable. The rest of our families have also been amazing, helping us gather information, taking the girls on play dates, and giving endless help around the house—another example of why (despite all that has happened) we feel so incredibly lucky.

One thing that has struck us in the e-mails you have sent is the number of people who have generously offered to be tested for bone marrow compatibility. While the doctors have told us that the chances of a friend or anyone other than a sibling matching Betsy are extremely remote, we want to encourage anyone who is interested to register as a donor anyway—not for Betsy—but for other people who are fighting blood cancers. As we get set to dip into the national registry looking for a stranger to help us, we feel it's important to raise awareness and encourage others to sign up for this valuable service.

If you are interested, please call the National Marrow Donor Program/Be The Match at 1-800-MARROW-2 for more information, or you can visit the following links:

- The Myths and Facts of Marrow Donation
  *http://bethematch.org/Join/Myths_and_Facts/Myths___Facts_*
  about_Donation.aspx
- Joining the Registry
  http://bethematch.org/Join/Join_the_Registry.aspx

Please consider signing up. It would be a wonderful way to help the cause, and you can literally save a life.

Until now, I had always thought of cancer as a single fight. You find out what you have, determine the course of treatment, and you beat it. What I realize now is that cancer isn't one fight, it's a constant battle. Every day we learn more about where we are, what is happening, and what the next step will be. Even days that you think will be relatively uneventful can test your strength and determination. You never know when something will shake you. But it's love, friendship, faith, and the support of those around you that help you steady yourself for the next challenge.

It's been a difficult few days. We've learned a lot, and much of what we have learned has been scary. But on the good side, we know what we're up against, and we have a pretty good idea of how hard we're going to have to fight.

I am so proud of Betsy for the way she is engaging in this battle. She has already taught me so much about inner strength and courage. There are times when she will hold my hand and I can feel the fear inside me start to fade. But even as she braces for the fight, she continues to display the caring, generous, and loving spirit that so many of you mention in your messages to her. She's not afraid to cry with people, and moments later she will have everyone laughing. And when Julia and Molly are in the room with her, you can often hear the laughter throughout the house. I am so thankful to have all three of them for this journey.

· · · · · · · · · · · · · · · · ·

CaringBridge Update: Saturday, June 18, 2005

In recent days there have been some positive developments in our battle and in our movement toward a bone marrow transplant.

First, Betsy's ankle is significantly better to the point where she can get out of bed, eat meals downstairs with us, and even take short walks outside. She went to the park a couple days ago with her mom and the girls, and while she feels a little weak, getting out and doing some normal activities is a huge boost. There is still a lot of leg pain from the Gleevec and she has good days and bad days, but just seeing her uplifts our spirits, and Julia and Molly love being able to play with Mommy again.

The second piece of good news is that we have a potential bone marrow donor for Betsy. He is being approached now to make sure that he is still willing and able to contribute, so we are crossing our fingers that everything will work out.

Finally, blood work from yesterday shows Betsy is definitely headed in the right direction. Her platelet count had been dangerously high and is now normal. The blast cell count in her blood continues to register zero—another great sign. We'll have two more blood tests next week to monitor things, and then a bone marrow biopsy the week after that will tell a more complete story.

Right now Betsy is responding well to the Gleevec, but according to the doctor, the average amount of time that Gleevec is effective on patients in blast crisis CML is eight weeks. That is our window of time to get a transplant done. If the Gleevec stops working, Betsy will have to do inpatient chemo to control the CML and will have to recover from that before we can do a transplant. This could delay things by a month or more, and would be much more difficult on her system. So if you're looking for something to visualize, here's what we're focused on:

1. The Gleevec needs to continue to get rid of the blast cells in Betsy's marrow.

2. The bone marrow donor needs to be willing and able to donate.

If the next bone marrow biopsy shows a blast cell count of less than 5 percent *and* the bone marrow donor comes through, we will move immediately to schedule the transplant, hopefully sometime in July.

Last week we asked the doctor if there would be some time before the transplant when the medicine would be working and we could have some quality time at home. He told us, "This IS your quality time. Don't wait for it."

It was an eye-opening statement. Since then Betsy has been out of bed whenever she has the energy and can tolerate the pain. Having her up and about brightens the entire house. Her energy and strength leave no doubt that this CML has met its match.

On the way home from the doctor yesterday we put on a "fight music" CD that I made for Betsy and she immediately started dancing (as only Betsy can) to Survivor's "Eye of the Tiger." I was laughing so hard I was in tears.

This is a strange journey. We have no context or experience to help us on the way and so we are learning as we go. We are trying not to look too far down the road. We are simply focused on the next step, and knowing you are behind us has helped us move forward confidently.

· · · · · · · · · · · · · · · · ·

CHAPTER 8

. . . .

Awe and Wonder

Once Betsy was on the Gleevec and we determined it was doing its job, we started a race against the clock. Because Betsy was in blast crisis, we knew she was not going to stay in remission very long. Our doctor's best guess was that it was going to be a matter of months before her blood counts would start to go up again.

So, in that limited amount of time we needed to:

- keep Betsy healthy
- build her strength emotionally and physically to prepare her for the transplant
- find a donor for her who would be a suitable match.

Each of these tasks could be difficult on its own, but accomplishing them all at the same time was particularly challenging.

Keeping Betsy physically healthy meant keeping her away from groups of people, taking extra precautions with hand washing and other germ control, and making sure she got enough rest.

On the other hand, her emotional strength required social interaction with friends, quality time with her family, and being out of bed as much as possible to make the most of those days when she was feeling pretty good.

Finally, on the donor front, we were told Betsy had a fairly common marrow type, so we thought finding a donor would be relatively easy. Unfortunately, there are so many variables to finalizing a donor it can take a lot longer than anticipated.

Finding a bone marrow donor is much more difficult than finding a blood donor. Marrow donation relies on human leukocyte antigen (HLA) typing to match patients and donors. HLAs are proteins that your immune system uses to decide which cells belong in your body and which cells should be attacked. They are not related to blood type. They are associated with your genetic makeup.

There are many HLA markers, but scientists have isolated ten that are the most important for a BMT match. If a minimal level of match can't be located, doctors can't proceed with a transplant. The closer the match, the better chance a patient has for surviving the transplant. Doctors refer to the match using numbers. A "6 of 8" match is minimally acceptable. A "10 of 10" is a perfect match. Where you fall in between this spectrum will impact how your body responds to the transplant and what your chances are for a relapse of the cancer.

In attempting to locate a donor, Be The Match scans its registry lists and international donor lists for potential matches, selecting a handful of the most promising. They reach out to those individuals to find out if they are still willing to donate, and if they could come in soon for a blood test to verify the match.

For weeks on end at our clinic appointments, we would receive slight variations on the same update:

- We reached out to five potential donors.
- So far, one has responded and is submitting a blood test to verify the match.
- We hope to have the results back soon so we can set a timeline for the transplant.

We would get our hopes up for the match, only to learn at our next visit that Be The Match was reaching out to a *new* batch of potential donors. We never knew why potential donors didn't work out. Maybe they proved to be less than ideal matches. Maybe they got cold feet and decided not to donate. All we knew is that the search was continuing, and the clock was ticking.

Luckily the other news we received during this time was excellent. Betsy's first bone marrow biopsy after starting on Gleevec showed *no* blast cells. In my book, this qualified as a miracle, considering her marrow was around 20 percent blast cells before she started treatment. The Gleevec was doing its job very well. As long as we could find a donor in time, Betsy would be ready for transplant.

The initial target date for the transplant was set for the first week in August, assuming the Gleevec would continue to work until then. Unfortunately our quest for a donor pushed the timeline back over and over again.

As the process continued, we became acutely aware of the need for bone marrow donors. Every time we went to the clinic, we would see a waiting room full of people going through treatment. Many of them were small children. Many of them would need a transplant.

We decided to fill the time that we were waiting for a donor by organizing our own bone marrow donor drive. One of our best friends lost his brother to leukemia, and his family foundation offered to help us conduct a registration drive.

As we started to raise awareness of the drive among family and friends, we stressed the fact that the drive was *not* an attempt to find a donor for Betsy. We didn't want anyone signing up under false pretenses. The chances of someone we know matching her would have been almost zero, and we were already far enough down the path that people registering at our event wouldn't be in a position to help her even in the unlikely event of a match.

This drive was not *for* Betsy, but it was driven by her experience. We wanted to do something to help other people whose lives are depending on finding a donor.

Heading into the donor drive, we were told that getting one hundred people registered over the course of the two days would be a great turnout. We ended up registering 143 people!

Betsy and I were able to be at the drive for the majority of the time, and we came away truly inspired. We got to see a lot of friends, and we reconnected with some people we hadn't seen in years. We also got to talk with a number of people whose lives have been impacted by cancer. It meant a lot to share stories and to learn from each other's experiences.

When it was all over, Betsy and I thought about how amazing it would be if even one person from our drive eventually matched someone in need.

Around this time, Betsy and I would sometimes talk about silver linings and the positive things we could draw from her experience. While it was an emotional and scary time, we realized we were already witnessing a number of silver linings that would surely stay with us long after the storm cleared.

One silver lining is that while we always enjoyed being together, we came to appreciate just how special time together is. Whether we were driving to a nice dinner in my parents' convertible with the top down, or simply curling up together to watch a movie, each moment took on new meaning and a new importance that I don't think will ever fade.

The other silver lining was a welcome reminder about how incredible people are. We are blessed with wonderful family and friends, and it's important to remember that.

One evening during this stretch, Betsy and Julia were reading stories in Julia's room for nap time when Julia looked up and noticed a rainbow on her ceiling. The sun was shining in and hitting a CD on her windowsill, reflecting onto the ceiling in a bright spectrum of colors. Julia stared at it—her eyes wide with amazement—and said, "I've never seen that before."

I loved the look of awe and wonder, and her appreciation of what seemed like a small miracle happening in her room. I could relate to that feeling. Whether it was watching Molly learn to walk, laughing harder and harder with each step, or it was marveling at Betsy's strength as she prepared to march into battle, I suddenly felt like there were miracles all around me.

. . . .

CaringBridge Update: Tuesday, July 26, 2005

Betsy's quest for a bone marrow donor is still on hold. We didn't get the results back on Thursday so at this point we still have two 6 of 8 donors identified. Again, that's a good enough match to move ahead, but we would like to have an even better match if at all possible. Three other blood tests are still being analyzed, and we have our fingers crossed.

The good news is that we now officially have a plan of action. We are going to wait until August 3 when the results from these other blood tests will be in. If we have a 7 or 8 match at that point, we'll move with that one. If we don't, we'll take the best 6 of 8 donor we have and proceed.

Given this deadline, we are at a critical stage for your thoughts and prayers. Any energy you can send around those three blood samples, focusing on a lucky 7 or 8 coming through, would be very much appreciated.

It's difficult to wait on these results knowing that we need to get the transplant done while the Gleevec is still working, and we don't know how long that will be. Betsy has blood tests twice a week and things have been looking good lately. Still, we can't afford to keep waiting on donors, so it was good to finally draw a line in the sand to make a decision and get things moving forward. We're still hoping to get the transplant done before the end of August.

Betsy continues to feel good and, despite the anticipation of what's ahead, we can't help but feel grateful for this extended period of quality time pre-transplant. Whether it's a trip to the zoo, watching Aquatennial fireworks over the Mississippi, or just dinner as a family, I actually find myself stepping back in the moment and marveling at how lucky we are to have this time together.

As we continue to move forward, we have been inspired by stories of others who have faced similar challenges. We've heard from a number of people who have faced cancer, gone through bone marrow transplants, and who have emerged from the challenge stronger than ever.

We are determined to add our own chapter to this volume of success stories.

· · · · · · · · · · · · · · · · ·

CHAPTER 9

. . . .

Kindness

As Betsy and I mentally prepared for the transplant, and tried to soak in as much quality family time as possible before that day, I became more and more thankful for all the ways in which our team of supporters was helping us along.

Two of our friends immediately started a "dinner sign-up" list when they heard about Betsy's diagnosis. They had meals arranged three times a week (to allow us to finish up leftovers and keep food from piling up). The meal deliveries were incredibly helpful, allowing us to spend our time taking care of Betsy, Molly, and Julia instead of grocery shopping and meal planning.

We received other spontaneous acts of kindness as well. One day a group of friends showed up with mulch, yard bags, rakes, and gloves, and in one day did our entire spring yard cleanup. Betsy was in a vulnerable state at the time, so she couldn't come out to help. By the end of the day, when Betsy was finally able to make her way out to say "thank you," the garden was fully weeded and planted, the yard was free of debris, and the tears in Betsy's eyes showed how much the support of her friends was helping Betsy as she worked to regain her strength and her health.

Shortly after Betsy's diagnosis, a group of friends from my work sent over a delivery of toys for Molly and Julia, gas cards to help me with my trips to and from the hospital, and a note that they had arranged a lawn service to mow our lawn all summer. Another friend arranged to have a massage therapist come to the house to give Betsy a massage.

But it wasn't just the big gestures of support that made a difference. Sometimes it was as simple as a word or two of support.

I know it can be difficult to know how to engage people who are facing a difficult time. Do you reach out to them to offer help, or do you grant them some space and privacy? Do you bring it up when you see them on the street? Or do you wait for them to bring it up? Where can you make a difference when they are faced with such a profound and difficult time in their lives?

Before Betsy's diagnosis I didn't have a clue as to how to help when I heard about people facing illness. I felt awkward bringing the topic up in conversation. I would sometimes send a note, but I was never sure a person in that situation would really want me to insert myself into his or her life even if I was trying to help.

Now I realize there are countless ways to help, and the most important thing you can do is to simply let others know you are thinking about them.

I vividly remember a moment soon after the diagnosis, on one of my first days back at work. It was near the end of the day, and a colleague stopped by my desk.

He stood there for a second and didn't say anything. Then he sat down and still said nothing. He looked like he had tears in his eyes.

Finally he said, "I heard about your wife...and...I'm not really very good at this. I don't really know what to say. But I wanted to stop by and just tell you...I hope she's doing okay, and we're hoping everything works out."

He stopped talking. I could tell he was having a hard time knowing what to say. I gave him a brief update about the situation and thanked him for stopping by. He looked relieved to get up and go.

I know he felt nervous about stopping by to see me, and he didn't want to say the wrong thing. But really, there wasn't a right or wrong to anything he said. It simply meant a lot to me to have him stop by.

To this day, when I hear about someone facing an illness or hardship, I think back to that moment and how my colleague's willingness to come over and say something meant so much to me. I may not always know what to say, or how to say it, but even a small gesture can make a big difference.

As we began to wrap our minds around the idea of a bone marrow transplant and an extended hospital stay, Betsy and I both knew that one of the hardest parts of the procedure would be separating from Julia and Molly.

Our first concerns were how to explain Mommy's absence, and how to keep their lives as normal as possible throughout Betsy's time away. We knew the girls could visit, but that was going to be a poor substitute for having Mom around every day.

I also knew that while I would be able to spend time with the girls every day, I would not be able to be "present" for them in the way I would want to be all the time.

The second concern centered around Betsy. To be that sick, and that scared, and to be separated from the two most important people in your life—we knew that would take an emotional toll.

As we first started to try to think of ways to ease this separation, Liz, one of Betsy's friends, came up with a plan.

Liz and her sister, Margaret, decided to make quilts—a large one for Betsy and small ones for Julia and Molly. With the help of Betsy's mom, they sent quilt squares out to Betsy's friends and family across the country, asking them to trace their hands on the square and to sign their names. Liz and Margaret sewed the squares together into a beautiful quilt, a visible show of support and love for Betsy to take to the hospital.

Betsy's quilt included handprints from Julia and Molly, our parents, uncles, aunts, cousins, friends, and me. Molly and Julia's quilts had handprints from Betsy, their friends, and me.

Liz and Margaret presented the finished quilts to Betsy and the girls not long before Betsy's transplant. They were beautiful. Betsy read over all the names and placed her hand on each square. This quilt would become a topic of conversation with the nurses who cared for Betsy in the hospital, as they would stop and admire the handprints and signatures.

Julia and Molly were happy to get their quilts too. And there were a number of times when Betsy was in the hospital when I would pull those quilts up to the girls' chins at night as they slept. I would nestle Betsy's handprint up to their faces, and whisper to them, "Your mommy loves you so much. She's fighting so hard. She will be home soon."

I don't know if it had any impact on Julia and Molly, but it felt good to be able to have part of Betsy with the girls every night as they slept.

CHAPTER 10

. . . .

Searching for Signs

One of the most disconcerting things that happened to me in the wake of Betsy's diagnosis was that thoughts of Betsy's mortality started to creep into my consciousness.

I tried to keep these thoughts at bay. We were legitimately optimistic and hopeful for a full recovery, so why did these thoughts keep prying their way into my brain?

Sometimes the strangest things would get me thinking about the possibility that Betsy might not make it.

One time I remember buying a new carton of Q-tips at the store. As I put them away in the bathroom I noticed the box had five hundred swabs inside. I wondered, briefly, whether Betsy would still be alive the next time I had to buy Q-tips. Just the thought sent a shiver through me. I shook my head and cleared my mind. But to this day, every time I look at a carton of Q-tips, I have a flashback to that day.

Another time, I remember visiting the Minnesota Landscape Arboretum and enjoying a beautiful day with Julia and Molly. As we walked around the grounds, it popped into my head that this was such a beautiful location it would be perfect to dedicate a bench in Betsy's memory if she didn't make it through the transplant.

I never dwelled on these thoughts. I pushed them out of my head as quickly as they entered, but I couldn't get rid of them altogether.

Sometimes I felt guilty when I had one of these moments, like I wasn't being strong enough and I was letting negativity in. But I finally decided that these thoughts were only natural. The fact was, there was a chance Betsy wouldn't make it, no matter how positive our attitudes were, or how hard she fought. I knew it was a possibility, so to deny it meant suppressing my feelings.

As long as I didn't let these thoughts consume me, perhaps they were giving me an outlet, a release to the pressure that was building as I tried to be a model of strength and positivity.

All I know is that these thoughts remained just on the edge of my day-to-day perspective, in the peripheral vision of my consciousness. On those occasions when I would briefly focus on them, I often pulled myself back feeling more determined, and in a way more confident, that Betsy wasn't going down that path.

In the uncertain days leading toward Betsy's bone marrow transplant, it was easy to let my mind wander in other ways. I looked for signs of hope. Not surprisingly, we received one, thanks to our daughters.

A couple weeks before the proposed transplant date, Julia found a caterpillar in the back yard. We put it in a "caterpillar house" and kept it in the backyard. A few days later, it transformed into a chrysalis.

Julia and Molly stared, wide-eyed, at the dark mass, hanging from a twig inside the house. Each day they would check to see if anything changed, but day after day there was no noticeable progress.

While the girls focused on the developments inside their bug house, Betsy and I were focusing on another type of progress. Every few days we checked in with our liaison at the National Marrow Donor Program to see if we had secured a match for Betsy. Over and over again we were told they were still reaching out to people, still analyzing matches, still waiting for the one match that would make our transplant a "go."

Then, finally, we got the call we were waiting for. Blood work had confirmed the match for Betsy, and the donor had agreed to go through with the procedure. Betsy was finally, officially, scheduled for her transplant!

As we celebrated this development, we went outside and heard cries of delight from Julia. After weeks of dormancy, her caterpillar had officially transformed! She led us over to the bug house to show off a beautiful butterfly. It had just emerged from the chrysalis and was slowly opening and closing its shimmering black and blue wings.

During our many visits to the Blood and Marrow Transplant Clinic, Betsy and I had noticed that there were butterfly drawings framed in most of the rooms. The staff explained that butterflies are a symbol of the transformation that happens with a bone marrow transplant. Patients enter the "cocoon" of the BMT unit and emerge transformed, with new life.

We couldn't help but interpret it as a sign of hope that our butterfly emerged on the day we confirmed Betsy's donor. As we released the butterfly from the bug house and watched it fly away, I felt my spirits lift in anticipation of the transformation and renewal now in motion for Betsy.

CHAPTER 11

. . . .

The Pieces Are in Place

. . . .

CaringBridge Update: Friday, August 5, 2005

As of today, the wheels are officially in motion taking us toward Betsy's bone marrow transplant and a cure for her leukemia. The blood samples that were being analyzed over the last week did not yield the 7 of 8 or 8 of 8 match we were hoping for, so we're moving ahead with a 6 of 8 match. It's important to remember, a 6 match is very good—until recently this was considered a perfect match. We can succeed with a 6…and so we will.

With this news, an entire timeline snaps into place. Betsy will begin her outpatient physical work-up on Monday, undergoing numerous tests throughout the week to make sure she's physically ready for the transplant. At the same time, we will be educated about all aspects of the road ahead to help us mentally prepare for the journey.

On the following Monday, August 15, Betsy will be admitted to the hospital to start aggressive chemotherapy and radiation treatment to knock out all of her marrow, wiping the slate clean to prepare her for the new marrow from her donor.

While all of this is happening here in Minnesota, somewhere in Europe the second part of this equation is moving forward as well.

One of our new favorite people in the world is a young man or woman (we don't know which) who is living somewhere in Europe (we don't know where). All we know is that this person is willing to donate to help save Betsy's life. This donor will go through a physical on Monday, and if he or she is healthy, his or her stem cells will be taken on August 23 or 24. The cells will be transported back to Minnesota, personally delivered by someone from our clinic who will fly out and back to be sure everything happens properly.

August 24 or 25 will be designated day "zero," when the donor cells will be transfused into Betsy's blood stream and will find their way into her bones to hopefully set up shop and start producing healthy blood cells for her.

If you stop and think about all the pieces that have to come together across the globe to make this thing happen, it's pretty amazing. Betsy and I are already looking forward to the day when we can personally thank this person in Europe who, with the simple act of signing up for the registry, ended up touching our lives in such a significant way.

It was an odd feeling going to the doctor today—a mix of anticipation and anxiety. There's something surreal about going to an appointment and HOPING that we will be able to schedule a bone marrow transplant. In a way, the fact that Betsy has been feeling so good lately has helped us take our minds off of the challenges ahead. Today served as a cold splash of water on the face and a big reality check. Not only is this transplant going to happen, it's going to happen soon!

With ten days left before she starts chemo, we're trying to get everything prepared and organized while still enjoying as much time as we can as a family before her extended hospital stay. Betsy continues to feel very good, which has allowed us to get out and have a lot of fun over the last weeks.

When we received the official word that the transplant is scheduled, it was sobering, but the person who seemed most ready for the fight was Betsy. The look in her eyes as we were talking about the next steps gave me strength, knowing that this CML doesn't stand a chance against her. Betsy is an inspiration to me.

Please continue your thoughts and prayers. And remember to send some positive thoughts in the general direction of Europe to the man or woman who is going in for a physical on Monday not knowing how many people are thankful for his or her generosity.

. . . .

CaringBridge Update: Wednesday, August 17, 2005

Tomorrow we officially embark on Betsy's journey to recovery when we check into the hospital at 6:30 a.m. After weeks of anticipation waiting for a donor and getting test after test done, now that the moment is here, it feels so sudden. We know we need to move as quickly as possible, but it's so hard to believe that after tonight, Betsy won't be sleeping at home for at least a few weeks.

The only procedure tomorrow is the installation of a Hickman catheter, a tube that will be inserted through a vein and into Betsy's heart. This catheter will be used to draw blood from now on, and to administer chemotherapy, medication, and the actual bone marrow transplant. The good news is that she won't have to be pricked with needles anymore. The disconcerting part is…well…having a tube inserted that leads directly to her heart. It's actually a fairly routine procedure, and is going to make things much easier through the transplant and recovery.

Tomorrow is officially day (-7). We're on a countdown to day (0) when the transplant will happen. Between now and then, Betsy will get massive doses of chemotherapy and total body radiation to try to eliminate all of the cancer cells in her body. They're going to essentially eliminate her immune system and start over with a clean slate.

The timing is definitely tight. Betsy's last bone marrow biopsy showed 1 percent blast cells. Anything below 5 percent is fine for moving ahead with the transplant, but the mere fact that the blast cells are showing up again demonstrates the urgency of getting the process moving.

Many of you have asked what you can do for Betsy while she's in the hospital. The most important thing you can do is to send thoughts and prayers, e-mails, cards, and notes on the CaringBridge site.

A few important things to note:

Please do not send plants, flowers, or balloons to Betsy. They don't allow any plants or flowers in the bone marrow transplant ward for fear of spreading infection. Latex balloons are also forbidden, and because of the size of the rooms, it's probably best to not have balloons of any kind.

Please don't send food to Betsy in the hospital. We won't know from day to day what she will be able to eat, or what she'll feel like eating. The effects of the chemo, radiation, and transplant could make having food in the room a little unpleasant.

Betsy can't have any visitors while she's in the hospital other than immediate family. Again, the biggest risk with a transplant is the risk of infection, and the more people visit, the greater the risk.

This is a very scary and anxious time, but it's also a relief to finally be charging into this process while Betsy's still in a good position for a successful transplant.

Other news on the transplant: We found out a little more about Betsy's bone marrow donor. He is a nineteen-year-old man somewhere in Europe. When we heard this, we marveled at the maturity and perspective that would drive someone to register as a donor at that age. We are so thankful for his generosity, and hope that we can thank him in person someday.

The only complication right now is that both Molly and Julia are sick, running fevers and feeling pretty lousy. The timing is not good, because if Betsy gets sick, the entire timeline gets delayed. Betsy has been trying to keep a distance to be safe, but it's difficult to pass up cuddle time with the girls when a hospital stay is right around the corner. They're starting to feel better now, and Betsy feels fine, so we should be okay moving ahead.

On the more positive side, the last week has brought further evidence of just how wonderful our friends and family are, and how lucky we are despite this challenge. Betsy and I were able to attend a prayer service last week where around one hundred people showed up to offer support. Looking out at the pews, we were overwhelmed and humbled by the outpouring of love. We feel like we are part of a big team that is rallying around one cause: the elimination of Betsy's CML! It's a great team, and it's a winning team.

Today I got home from work to the sight of Betsy in a new, very short hairdo—a sort of a "transition-do" to ease the path to having no "do" at all. She looks great. She's been packing all day, and we just finished putting the girls to bed for one last time as a family before embarking on this next phase. Through the stories, and Julia's questions about why Mommy has to go to the hospital, and Betsy's explanation about her "sick blood" needing strong medicine, Betsy was as radiant and loving as ever. I sat and watched, and marveled at her strength and grace, and it made me feel so confident that Betsy's cancer has met its match and is about to face its last stand.

· · · · · · · · · · · · · · · · ·
_____

Journal Entry – August 21, 2005

We've made it to day (-3) without incident. For all the turmoil going on inside Betsy's body right now, there's an atmosphere of serenity around her. It's easy to forget about the seriousness of the situation, but at the same time it is always bubbling just below the surface.

Last night we were relaxing and watching a movie when, all of a sudden, the fans for the filtration system went out. We didn't know this until a nurse came in to tell Betsy to put her mask on until further notice.

Just at that moment, Betsy also had a sudden dizzy spell; when she stood up, she could feel her heart beating. Just that quickly the relaxation of the evening turned to concern and fear. Do I need to alert someone? Is your heart still pounding? Does it feel like it did when your potassium was low?

Everything was fine. The fans came back on. Betsy's mask came off. Her heart stopped pounding and her vital signs were normal. Still, it was a reminder that things can (and will) turn on a dime.

It was four days ago that we left the house at 6:15 a.m. to check in to the hospital. The early morning departure was probably good. It muted the emotion of saying goodbye to Julia and Molly, at least a little bit. Being away from the girls will be one of the hardest parts of the coming weeks.

After check-in, as we walked back to the room where Betsy would be prepped for her Hickman catheter, I felt like we were in a movie—like we should be walking in slow motion like the astronauts in *The Right Stuff*, heading down the corridors to embark on the first launch into space.

The journey we're embarking on is just as awe inspiring, and I felt a similar sense of confidence walking through those halls. We're actually starting down the path. We're officially starting the fight. We've got a great team behind us. We're going to succeed.

The catheter went in with no issues, and the discomfort is more than outweighed by the benefits of not getting stuck with more needles.

After the procedure, we had to stay in the catheterization area for a few hours waiting for Betsy's room to be ready.

While we were waiting, I heard a "code blue" announcement for 4B, the bone marrow transplant unit. The nurses told me there were two incidents going on in 4B that were delaying our move into our room. I couldn't help trying to imagine what these "incidents" were, hoping the results were okay, and praying that our time in 4B would not include any mention of "code blue" or similar issues.

It was early afternoon when we were led to the room. Walking in was reminiscent of walking into a freshman year dorm room. There's anxiety knowing this is going to be home for a while. There's inevitable disappointment at first.

"Wow, this is small. How are we going to fit everything in here and be comfortable?"

Then there's a shift to look at the positives.

"The view is nice. There's a nice window ledge bench for sitting. The closet's okay."

We don't have a choice. This is going to be our home, so why not turn it into a positive? We started to get settled.

One of the most remarkable things about the BMT is the people. The nurses and aides are so friendly and helpful. They put us at ease quickly. They smile a lot. They listen. They *want* to look at pictures of Molly and Julia, and they *want* to know about the handprints on Betsy's quilt. They take the time to explain things. They understand how important they are in terms of making our time here less scary and more comfortable.

When we checked into the BMT, a nurse named Kelly met us at the door and walked us to our room. She helped us get settled and started the check-in process. She was so pleasant and friendly I liked her immediately. Then another nurse came into our room, saw Kelly, and asked if she'd mind continuing to check us in while she helped another patient. Kelly gladly agreed.

That's when I realized that Kelly wasn't even assigned to our room. She was just stepping in to help while the nurse assigned to us was busy. Something about her cheerfulness and willingness to take on additional work to get us settled made me feel so good about the BMT. I immediately knew we were going to get great care here. I knew that the nurses and aides were in it for the right reason.

A couple days after we checked in, when I was at the kitchen getting Betsy something to drink, I ran into Kelly again. She asked how we were doing.

"We're doing pretty well so far," I replied. Then I paused and thought about her job and the intensity that I had witnessed in just a short time on the unit. I asked her a question.

"So, in terms of units for being a nurse, is this considered a *good* assignment?"

"This is an amazing place," she said with no hesitation.

I had to ask more.

"Why? It seems like it would be pretty tough."

Kelly paused briefly and looked at me with a slight smile.

"Every day when I come to work, I get the chance to see a miracle happen."

I am so thankful that there are people like Kelly, who can give their heart to a demanding and emotionally challenging job every day. I can already tell it takes someone really special to see the miracles on 4B.

The attending physician for the next couple of weeks is Dr. Greg Vercellotti. He's the kind of doctor who starts out asking about your life, family, and work before getting into medicine and treatment. He put us at ease immediately. We look forward to seeing him each morning simply because he's a nice man and he's interesting to talk with.

The other day he spent at least a half hour telling us about his career, his time as the dean of the medical school, his research, and his philosophy of care. He even found time to talk a little baseball, which I particularly enjoyed.

He has perspective gained from studying history and philosophy. He's a collaborator who doesn't get caught up in ego or hierarchy. He's exactly the kind of doctor I would want looking after Betsy right now.

Betsy started chemo at around 10:00 the morning of day (-6). It's a little strange how casual and uneventful the start of chemo is, simply starting a drip into her catheter. At the same time, it was a momentous occasion, and that recognition soon hit us. We held hands and had a moment of silence/prayer/thanks for this moment when the formal attack on her cancer cells began. About two hours later, the Cytoxan was fully into her system, assaulting her cells. Aside from a little lightheadedness, Betsy's appearance, demeanor, and spirit belied the nature of the assault on her system.

This dichotomy between the internal battle and external serenity has marked all of our time on 4B thus far. Betsy endured both doses of chemo with no nausea and no real side effects. She started total body radiation at 8:00 yesterday morning and appeared to breeze through what can be an emotionally challenging procedure. She's nearly halfway done with radiation now and other than fatigue and some night sweats we've seen no ill effects. She's even been able to walk on the treadmill in the room.

Radiation treatment is one of those procedures that I had heard about many times, but had no idea of what it is really like.

Before Betsy checked in to the hospital, she had to visit the radiation therapy unit for a "fitting," where they had her sit in the radiation room and get measured so they could program the machines to deliver the right amount of radiation.

I went into the room as they explained the procedure. The room looked pretty similar to what I had imagined: a large white machine, a standard procedure table, and everything was white.

What I hadn't imagined were all the accessories that were lined up on shelves in the room. There were plaster casts of different parts of the body, torsos, heads and necks, hips and legs. I asked what they were for, and the technician said they were to help make sure patients sit in the exact same position from session to session so they can pinpoint the exact location of the radiation each time.

I asked if Betsy was going to need a cast and he said, "No." For total body radiation you don't need a cast, because the radiation is supposed to hit everywhere.

The tech had Betsy sit down on the table with her knees pulled up to her chest. He then pulled out some duct tape and taped her feet to the table. Her hands were placed on her shins and then taped as well.

The tech explained that the position of her arms and hands is very important, because they need to try to shield Betsy's lungs from the radiation. Everything in her body, all of her organs were going to be hit—but they wanted to at least shield her lungs as much as possible.

They took measurements of Betsy sitting in this position. They explained that they do it from one side, and then swing the table around to do the other side. They have the radio playing and she can request a station, but she really just needs to sit still.

I think watching the fitting finally drove home to me how potent full body radiation is, and how mentally draining it can be to sit in an awkward position alone in a room with nothing to do but think about what is happening to you.

When the time came for her radiation sessions, Betsy seemed to handle everything fairly easily, but I knew once again there had to be more below the surface. Courage is an amazing thing, but I tried to pay extra attention to Betsy's needs on our way to and from the radiation room.

· · · · · · · · · · · · · · · ·

CaringBridge Update: Sunday, August 21, 2005

Today is officially day (-3) and Betsy is doing great. There's no way of predicting how anyone will react to chemo and radiation, so we're counting any day that she feels good as a gift.

I've been staying at the hospital with her and we've been able to make the most of it. We listen to a lot of music, read a lot, and have been able to watch a couple of movies. So far her appetite is good, food still tastes good to her, and her spirits are high.

We have been extremely happy with the care Betsy is getting. The nurses in the BMT ward are amazing. They are very good at taking the time to explain things to us, and they have very optimistic and engaging personalities. This is the type of care Betsy responds to, so it's a great fit.

Julia, Molly, and Betsy's mom have all been battling colds, so they haven't been able to visit yet, but they're getting better. It will be so great to bring the girls in. Betsy misses them so much.

Betsy has been amazing to watch so far. She's able to laugh at the absurdities, such as the way her new short haircut gets messy overnight and makes her look a little like Billy Idol when she wakes up in the morning. Despite the difficulty of the situation and the scary nature of what's going on, we're doing our best to enjoy this time together.

· · · · · · · · · · · · · · · ·

CHapTer 12

· · · · · · · · · · · · · ·

Transplant Day!

· · · · · · · · · · · · · · · ·

CaringBridge Update: Wednesday, August 24, 2005
A call to action! We just found out that Betsy's donor cells are in town and are being processed as we speak. We were told yesterday that they wouldn't be here until tonight, meaning the transplant would take place after midnight—but it turns out they're here now!

They're prepping Betsy for the transplant, which will probably take place in about two hours, sometime between noon and 1:00 p.m. central time.

Please take a moment this morning and again in a couple hours to send extra positive thoughts and prayers to Betsy. Think about those new cells moving into her body, liking it there, and setting up shop to start producing blood cells for her.

We've been waiting for this for a long time, and now that it's here we've got quite a mix of nerves and excitement. This is the big step to a cure—and it all begins now!!

We'll send an update later today. Thanks to all of you for your support. It makes such a difference!

· · · · · · · · · · · · · · · ·

CaringBridge Update: Wednesday, August 24, 2005
Today was a day that we will never forget. In a sense, Betsy was reborn at 1:20 p.m. when a bag of stem cells from a nineteen-year-old man in Germany was transfused into Betsy's body. August 24 will now be Betsy's "second birthday," and in many ways it was as miraculous as her first.

Originally we were told the transplant was going to take place after midnight tonight. At around 9:45 this morning, we were told there was a change in plans. It turns out that our donor overachieved. Usually it takes two sessions to get enough stem cells from the donor for the transplant. Ours was able to provide more than enough in one session. This allowed them to get the cells out on an earlier flight.

Betsy called her family and told them the new time. They all came to the hospital to be with her. Around 1:00 p.m. the nurse brought the cells into the room. We took a few pictures of Betsy holding the bag. They hooked her up and started the transplant at 1:20—a moment that we will toast for years to come.

Many people have told us that the transplant is a little anticlimactic after all the buildup. After all, it's really just a cell transfusion. Even so, we were struck by the occasion.

As soon as the new cells began to enter Betsy's catheter, her lips started to tingle, followed closely by a rush of warmth that washed over her entire body. Betsy said she felt like her body was 150 degrees even though her temperature never went above normal. It was an extremely powerful moment. There was a sense that we were witnessing the greatest miracles of science and God working simultaneously to cure Betsy of her cancer. It was all over in about forty minutes, but in that short amount of time, Betsy was literally given new life.

When you think about the journey that Betsy's new stem cells took in a twenty-four-hour period, it's mind-boggling. Then, when you think that somehow those stem cells are going to find their way through Betsy's blood stream and into her bone cavities to set up shop and start producing blood cells, it's awe inspiring.

We've come a long way in the last week—two rounds of heavy chemo, four days of total body radiation, and a transplant. Betsy has been lucky to have no major side effects yet and her spirits have been high. Our medical care has been unbelievable—the nurses, our physician's assistant, the doctors, and the aides are amazing. We feel so lucky.

We know there are some hard days ahead. We're on day 0, and many people say days 8 through 14 are the toughest. We need to avoid any infections while her immune system is out of commission, and we need to hope and pray that these cells graft correctly in her bones to get her system running again. Still, we're happy to be off to a great start.

If you're looking for something to visualize, please think about the donor cells planting themselves snugly into Betsy's bones and starting to work. It's a lot like planting a garden and waiting for vegetables to grow. I'm confident the cells will find Betsy's bones to be a fabulous place to set up shop and be productive.

All morning Betsy and I were talking about how similar this day was to the days when our daughters were born. There's the anticipation, the uncertainty about when the big moment will arrive, the rush of adrenaline that accompanies new life, and the exhaustion and amazement that follow. I have to say I was as proud of her today as I was on the days when Molly and Julia were born. She embraced this moment, and fully appreciated the gift that we have been given by this amazing donor.

. . . .

Journal Entry – August 26 (Day 2)
Nothing could have possibly prepared me for the emotions of this day. Now that I have a moment to think and process, I have a new appreciation for what a bone marrow transplant represents. It is a miraculous process by many measures: logistical, scientific, physical, mental, and spiritual.

Logistical

To be able to coordinate the growth and harvesting of stem cells somewhere in Germany, and then to have them delivered, processed, and ready at the exact time that chemo and radiation have prepared Betsy's body to receive them is logistically incredible.

There were so many things that had to go right. The donor had to make it to his appointment. The person sent to transport the cells had to arrive and collect the package. The flight from Germany had to be on time. We even found ourselves sending positive thoughts to the driver taking them from the airport to the processing center. One car crash could upset the entire process.

The moment that the nurse came through the door with the bag of cells was so exciting. We stared at it almost like it was a newborn. Betsy gingerly held it for pictures before gently handing it back to the nurse.

Scientific

The science behind bone marrow transplant is also remarkable. Imagine the steps that were made and the challenges that had to be overcome for the first transplant nearly four decades ago. We're so grateful for the pioneers who paved the way, and for all of the research and science that gave us this chance for a cure.

Science is always improving. Gleevec has completely changed the landscape for CML. Antinausea drugs are making chemo and radiation at least more tolerable. We're benefiting from so many studies that have revolutionized cancer treatment from where it was even a half a decade ago.

Betsy is committed to do her part to help further the cause. She signed up for a number of tests, agreeing to provide extra blood samples for research throughout the transplant. She is also participating in a blind study comparing the effectiveness of two antifungal medications. We're hopeful these tests can help keep the momentum going as doctors work to deliver the knockout punch to CML and other cancers.

Physical

The physical nature of bone marrow transplant is difficult to get your mind around. On one hand it's very simple: the cells are transfused into Betsy's body through her catheter, just like they do when they need to give her blood or medication. But the nature of her physical transformation is deep and complex.

Betsy's immune system is being replaced. Her blood will have a different genetic makeup. While it appears that her donor had her same blood type, if he hadn't, Betsy's blood type would have changed. To completely replace *all* of your bone marrow, and thus your blood, is a physical feat that defies comprehension.

Mental

The mental side of BMT has a number of facets. The most obvious are fear and anxiety. How is my body going to react? Is it going to work? Is my body ready for this? Is the cancer gone?

The other side of the mental equation is more positive and hopeful. In Betsy's case, this is the side that ruled the day. We were focused on the donor and his life-saving gift. Who is he? What's his story? What happened to this nineteen-year-old to compel him to get on the registry? Does he have any idea how grateful we are for this gift?

Bone marrow transplants also call for mental strength—focus on the process and the goal. You need to balance living in the moment and concentrating on next steps with an awareness of the big picture and the ultimate goal.

Just like when a baseball manager tells his team not to get too high after a win or too low after a loss, we can't let a good day fool us into thinking this will be a breeze, and we can't let a bad day pull us into despair. It's all about keeping an eye on the prize and dealing with each of the steps to get there.

Spiritual

The most striking and perhaps surprising part of the transplant was the unmistakable spiritual side of the moment. As the transfusion was being hooked up and we watched the stem cells travel down the tube toward Betsy's catheter, we were all conscious of the fact that those weren't just cells, they were life.

When they entered Betsy's body, the sensation and warmth were startling at first, but afterward Betsy described it in a more reassuring way. She said it was like a "hug from God." A life-giving embrace.

No matter what the cause of the sensations Betsy felt, we knew the moment was bigger than the physical sensations she was feeling. We wished the donor could have been in the room. Anybody who experiences this would want to be called on to donate. It gives you a true understanding of the magnitude of this gift.

Right now in America, we are seeing a debate around the role of science versus religion. Politicians raise questions about evolution, and there are movements to teach "intelligent design" in schools.

I believe this debate does a disservice by asserting a supposed conflict between science and spirituality.

A bone marrow transplant is a perfect example of how the two are not at odds. It is science that brought us to the point where we can replace Betsy's bone marrow with donor stem cells. Science lets us understand CML and how to control and cure it. But if you ask any doctor how those donor cells know how to find their way through Betsy's body and into her bones to set up shop and produce blood cells, you'll get nothing but a shrug or a shake of the head, and a sense of the wonder and admiration that scientists still have for the intricate workings of the human body and the nature of life.

I believe science and spirituality are not at odds. In fact, the more we understand about science, the greater our appreciation might become for the miracles that surround us. I do know that both science and spirituality were in play at 1:20 p.m. on August 24 when Betsy's donor cells entered her body and gave her a second chance at life.

———————————

CHAPTER 13

. . . .

The Battle

Journal Entry – August 27 (Day 3)

We've been told by a number of people that the first ten days post-transplant are the hardest. I hope that's true.

Yesterday, after more than a week in the hospital with few issues to speak of, we got a reality check. Betsy woke up with a very sore mouth and throat, and, just like that, difficult days began.

At first Betsy was defiant, saying, "We're in a battle here. We knew I was going to get battered a little."

Then the pain was too bad to swallow and they started her on a little morphine. The rest of the day was nothing but fitful sleep interrupted only by the beep of Betsy self-administering morphine doses and sessions of terrible nausea.

I always get sad when morphine enters the picture. Not because I don't think it's necessary, but rather because it speaks to a scary state when a restless, sleepy haze is preferable to life without it.

We knew there would be a time in this process for morphine and feeding tubes, but things were going so well, and now the turn is so sudden.

Throughout this process, I've had people tell me that being the spouse of a cancer patient is in some ways more difficult than being the patient. I think that's an exaggeration. Fighting for your life and dealing with pain, nausea, fear, uncertainty, and separation from family and friends is about as tough as it gets.

But there are aspects of being a cancer spouse that are very difficult and hard to understand until you're living it.

Some of the difficulties are obvious—fear of losing someone you love (and all that entails), watching your wife endure treatments, and seeing the fear and pain on her face. There's also the stress of managing work, finances, home and hospital life, and sleeping at the hospital with the semi-comfortable cot and the constant interruptions to sleep.

But the toughest part of this role so far is what I'm feeling now: helplessness. Betsy is miserable, and there's nothing I can do about it. Words of encouragement ring hollow. Even speaking to Betsy can bring on more nausea. Offers to bring food, sorbet, ice cream, smoothies, soup, or crackers, always gets a mixed reaction. And even if Betsy feels like trying something, by the time I get it, she's back asleep, or her stomach no longer agrees with the choice.

When you love someone, you want to take her pain away. You want to make her happy and healthy. Right now I can't do that, and it's hard. I have no idea how long this will last, but it could be another week or so. When you think about what's going on inside of her body it makes sense that she would be miserable. I just keep looking for a way to bring some relief along the way.

Having a family member in the BMT unit enlists you in a strange fraternity. When I walk the halls I often see Vanessa's mom and dad. Vanessa is an eleven-year-old who was in our orientation and is on Betsy's exact transplant schedule. They're a really nice family, and they have been through the ringer. Vanessa has acute lymphoblastic leukemia (ALL) and went through major chemo (Gleevec, Cytoxin, Methotrexate, etc.). Five months after finishing chemo, she relapsed, so here they are.

Last night I was talking with her father about the difficult phase we've entered. Vanessa had had a tough day too. I then met a man whose sixteen-year-old son had just been readmitted for a sixth time with a fungal infection. He spoke with a veteran's perspective about the difficulty of days 0 to 14. He then told me his son had undergone a new procedure that only four other patients have ever had. All four of the others are now deceased, but his son is doing well. He's at day 98. Now, whenever I see him, I pull for them both. They're beating the odds, and I hope they can finally beat this.

There are so many milestones—transplant day...day 10...discharge day...day 100...it goes on and on.

Right now I'm just looking forward to crossing off day 3. And I'm hoping for some relief for Betsy tomorrow.

An interesting element of being a caregiver is that there are times when your ability to provide care, relief, or comfort is extremely limited. You can be at your loved one's side. You can hold her hand. You can tell her things will be okay. But none of that takes away the feelings of helplessness, or the loss of control.

During some particularly difficult stretches for Betsy, I sometimes compensated for these feelings with moments of superstitious thought. I would pretend I had some sort of cosmic level of control over a situation that, deep down, I knew was completely out of my hands.

Much like a baseball player who develops strange routines to try to break out of a slump, or who tries to repeat certain behaviors to maintain a hot streak, I started adjusting my actions and routines to try to "help" Betsy.

If Betsy had a good day and seemed to be improving, I would try to re-create my exact steps from the day before. How I brushed my teeth...the pattern I used when I was shaving my face...how I washed my hair in the shower...I focused on doing things the exact same way to keep Betsy's hot streak going.

On the other hand, when Betsy had a rough day, I would shake things up. I would switch the order of my morning routine. Perhaps I would shower before shaving. If things were really bad, I might brush my teeth left-handed.

My personality is far from compulsive, but I still found myself paying attention to my actions, and clinging to the thought that perhaps I could exert some control to keep Betsy on track.

I knew that how I shaved or tied my shoes had nothing to do with Betsy, just like I'm pretty sure a baseball manager knows that stepping on the baseline chalk on the way to the mound won't change the location of the next pitch. Still, I indulged these superstitions from time to time, figuring it couldn't hurt. After all, if a butterfly flapping its wings can cause a hurricane on the other side of the globe, maybe brushing my teeth left-handed could unleash forces that could help Betsy turn things in the right direction. I guess you never know.

. . . .

CaringBridge Update: Sunday, August 28, 2005
Betsy has been sleeping much of the last few days and hasn't been able to eat much of anything. They're nourishing her through her catheter. She did have a decent evening last night after a change in her pain medication, but today was another combination of pain and sleepiness.

We knew that the first couple weeks post-transplant were going to be tough, and they are living up to that billing. The full effect of the chemo and radiation are starting to emerge, and her low blood counts are contributing to the discomfort. Still, we are very optimistic. Please continue to visualize the stem cells planting themselves in her bones and starting to produce. That's the key right now.

. . . .

CaringBridge Update: Wednesday, August 31, 2005
Well, we've hit a patch in the road that is very difficult—once again a harsh reminder that victory in this battle will be hard earned.

One of the antirejection drugs that Betsy has been receiving can cause swelling in the mouth and throat—a very painful condition called mucositis. It is very difficult to control because her body has no white cells to fight it.

Betsy has a bad case, and it's making her fight very difficult right now. She got very little sleep last night because she has difficulty breathing when she lays her head back.

The doctors have been working to get this under control all day with limited success. Betsy is exhausted and has basically been hovering between being asleep and awake all day. Her breathing is okay, but sometimes labored.

She's just now getting her biggest stretch of sleep in a while, but it's something of a drug-induced, restless sleep. I'm hoping she can fall into a deeper sleep for the rest of the evening and night. She needs it.

The doctors are ready to take stronger action if her breathing becomes a problem, but we're hoping we won't have to go that direction. Suffice it to say, we're praying that things get under control so she can be more comfortable.

On the good side, earlier today we moved from our small room into a large room that opened up in our unit. It's about three times as big, so we finally have some space to move around.

We also had an exciting moment yesterday with the ceremonial shaving of Betsy's head. Betsy has officially joined the ranks of Sigourney Weaver, Demi Moore, and Natalie Portman as women who look fabulous with shaved heads. Julia came to the hospital to witness the occasion and declared, "Mommy, you have a nice head!" She was right.

Julia also painted a beautiful mural on Betsy's window with paints the hospital has on hand. Now that we're in a different room, she'll get to come back and paint an encore.

Betsy continues to be a strong fighter and to meet all challenges in such an admirable manner. It's just tough to see how hard she has to work.

· · · · · · · · · · · · · · · · ·

Journal Entry – September 5, 2005 (Day 12)
A lot has been happening over the last few days. These have been days I will never forget, even though I would like to.

Betsy's third dose of methotrexate resulted in an extreme case of mucositis that made it very hard for her to breathe. Tuesday night it was so bad I was afraid she was going to stop breathing.

The constricted airway made Betsy snore very loudly, so every time there was silence I would get nervous. The difficulty breathing made Betsy panic from time to time, and she was not able to sleep well because every time she fell asleep, she couldn't breathe.

By Wednesday morning, Betsy was in terrible shape. Her mouth and throat were so swollen she could hardly close her mouth. She was producing so much mucus they had to hook up a vacuum tube so she could suck it out of her mouth and throat. She could hardly speak. Every syllable required considerable effort. Her breathing was labored and at times seemed to stop, only to start up again with a loud snore.

The combination of pain medications (they switched her to Fentanyl after deciding she's allergic to morphine) and a lack of sleep kept Betsy hovering on the edge of consciousness, desperate to sleep, but scared to fall asleep and stop breathing.

This was a horrible day. Betsy was miserable. They decided to move us to a bigger room, which is nice, but they did it so they would have room for a ventilator and other equipment they would need if her breathing got worse.

I was told they were going to try one more step, a combination of steroids and an epinephrine nebulizer, and if that didn't work they were going to intubate her proactively rather than waiting for her airways to close and doing an emergency procedure.

Waiting for the drugs to work was difficult. It was a challenge to simply keep Betsy awake and coherent long enough to administer the nebulizer. I had to talk her through the sessions…

"Okay Betsy, deep breaths."

"You're doing great. Keep breathing."

"Keep breathing…just a little bit more."

"Betsy, you NEED to keep breathing…deep breaths!"

"Almost there…great job!"

I don't know that she could hear what I was saying, but my voice would stir her enough to wake her up and keep the medicine flowing into her throat and lungs.

They kept an oxygen monitor on Betsy's finger that would beep loudly if her levels got low, something that would periodically happen and would immediately send my heart rate up as I raced to see what was going on. I realized how serious her situation was when, in the middle of the night, the oxygen monitor went off and the nurse made it into the room and to Betsy before I got there from my bed. They were nervous. I was scared.

Betsy's breathing sounded awful and painful. The drugs gave her strange dreams and hallucinations. She would constantly pick at the blankets like she was picking up food to eat. She would pull at the oxygen monitor on her finger (causing more beeping). She would imagine different people in the room and shyly sit up and wave to them with her eyes closed. Sometimes she would talk in her sleep—usually quietly and incomprehensibly, but sometimes it was loud and clear. Even when she appeared awake and somewhat alert, a coherent sentence would take a turn midway through and become nonsensical.

Whenever she got too active, panicky, or would start to pull at her monitor, I would sit on her bed and hold her hand with both of mine and tell her she was fine and doing great. At other times I tried to stay away from her bedside because I soon figured out I could drive myself crazy watching her breathe, monitoring her oxygen levels, and trying to understand all of her mutterings and hallucinations.

I compare it to watching an infant breathe. If you watch closely you can start to panic with every twitch or skipped breath. I had to occupy myself to avoid that anxiety.

By Saturday, it was obvious Betsy was improving. Her breathing was better. She was adjusting to the pain medications and hallucinating less. She was able to talk. She walked for ten minutes on her treadmill and even pulled a few dance moves on her way back to her bed. It was a relief to see some of her old spark and personality.

By Sunday, Betsy was so much better they decided to give her the full final dose of methotrexate. This was good news because while it is a harsh drug, it's important in helping reduce graft-versus-host disease (GVHD).

GVHD is a common, usually necessary, and sometimes life-threatening side effect of a bone marrow transplant.

When you have a transplant, you create a completely new immune system. This immune system doesn't recognize its new body and will often attack cells or organs thinking they are intruders.

A little GVHD is a good thing, because the immune system will often target and wipe out any stray cancer cells that might remain in the body even after chemo and radiation. In this way, GVHD is critical in preventing a relapse of cancer. (Interestingly, this is why it's not good to get a transplant from an identical twin. The match is so good, there is no GVHD, and there is a high relapse rate.)

Too much GVHD is a really bad thing. If the new immune system starts attacking major organs, it can be fatal. Managing the amount of GVHD post-transplant is one of the most difficult aspects of a BMT, and that's why giving Betsy a full dose of methotrexate is important.

The new attending doctor felt Betsy could handle the final dose, and so far she is doing fine.

CHAPTER 14

. . . .

Small Victories

The role of caregiver is the ultimate "trial by fire" experience. Nobody plans to take on this role, and it's impossible to be prepared for all that it requires. You don't get any time to process the role or to plan ahead. All you can do is accept your role, try to do your best, and hope you won't let anything bad slip through the cracks along the way.

Admittedly, I had a distinct advantage in adjusting to my caregiver role in that Betsy's mom was able to move in and take over many day-to-day tasks around the house. Still, there were many times when I was faced with tasks that were difficult to juggle, or moments when the pressures of what was going on at the hospital, at work, and at home would build exponentially.

Often it was the little things that knocked me out of my comfort zone and made me rise to the occasion. For me, one of those unexpected challenges was, of all things, hair.

There was a moment, not long after Betsy checked into the hospital, when Julia came to me asking if I could put her hair in a binder.

It was a simple enough request. The problem was, I had never done it before. Betsy was the hair stylist in our family. I had seen her put Julia's hair in binders many times. I had never in my life attempted the maneuver.

Julia, of course, didn't know that. All she knew was that she wanted her hair out of her eyes, and she wanted a pink binder. Not wanting to disappoint her, I took the brush and the binder and did my best to replicate Betsy's hair technique. To my amazement, the result wasn't half bad.

I asked Julia to look in the mirror to see if it was okay. As she checked out my handiwork and nodded in approval, I felt a rush of pride that was far beyond what one should feel from the simple placing of a hair binder.

That binder request was, of course, just the beginning. Once Julia saw I could put a binder in, I started to get more complicated requests. Ponytails were a challenge, but I soon became pretty good at them. Pigtails were, to my chagrin, not a specialty.

One day, Julia asked for pigtails before school. I was running late but decided to give it a try. After multiple attempts, I pleaded with Julia to just go with one of my patented ponytails. She agreed. Unfortunately, I was off my game that morning. I walked Julia up to the door of school trying to straighten out the binder, to get the recalcitrant clumps of hair to fall in line with the rest, but to no avail. I sent her off to class hoping none of the other parents were noticing. That's when I saw the mom of one of Julia's friends.

She said, "Hi," and asked me how I was doing.

I sheepishly said things were going okay, but confessed that I had just sent Julia into class with a kind of ridiculous hairdo.

To my relief she just laughed and said, "I had the same issue this morning." She told me how her daughter wasn't cooperating and was demanding a different hairstyle, and how the result was kind of a disaster.

I immediately felt better, like maybe my hair anxiety wasn't as warranted as I thought. In fact, I felt more confident in my abilities, knowing that even seasoned professionals can have a bad morning.

It wasn't long before fixing the girls' hair became second nature to me. I never did conquer the pigtails, but I executed *one* moderately successful French braid, and I have successfully put both girls' hair into foam rollers (it took me more than an hour, but it worked).

Still, there are moments even today when I'm helping Julia or Molly with their hair and I think back to that initial request, the moment when the caregiver role became a hairstylist role, and I was able to rise to the occasion. It was a small victory, but it came at a time when I would take any kind of victory I could get.

. . . .

CaringBridge Update: Friday, September 9, 2005

It's now day 16 post-transplant.

When you're battling an illness, it's natural to judge your progress by how you're feeling. If you feel better today than you did yesterday, you must be improving. That's not the case in the days following a bone marrow transplant.

Betsy won't be able to start feeling better until her new stem cells start producing white blood cells. When her white counts come in, those cells will immediately start healing the pain in her mouth and throat and she'll make noticeable improvement. Her white counts may not start coming in for a few days, or even a week or so, so for the time being, all we can do is wait and take comfort in the fact that she is making incredible progress every day, even if she can't feel the effects yet.

Getting Betsy's white count back is the next major step in recovery, so if you're looking for something to visualize, please focus on this. We need those new stem cells, which are now planted comfortably in Betsy's bones, to start doing their job. We're confident that those are some special stem cells, so we're hopeful that they'll once again overachieve and bring Betsy some relief very soon.

We had another milestone this week, as Julia officially started preschool. I was so proud of her, watching her walk down the hallway to her classroom, showing her new backpack off to her new teacher. When I picked her up at the end of school, we immediately went to the hospital so she could tell Mommy all about her day. It was sad for Betsy to miss the first day, but as I watched Julia march into this new experience with confidence and enthusiasm, I couldn't help but think how much she's like her mother, tackling this new challenge with such a positive and uplifting attitude. I'm inspired by both of them.

. . . .

CHAPTER 15

. . . .

A Miracle

Every morning in 4B the nurses come in and take a blood sample for analysis. Primarily, they are looking to see if a patient's blood counts are coming in, which means the new stem cells are starting to produce blood cells.

They don't bother to check for the first six or seven days post-transplant because there's no chance of having counts then, but after that it becomes a daily ritual, and it is the BMT equivalent of panning for gold. The blood is drawn in the morning and analyzed for any trace of new cells while we anxiously wait for the day we can exclaim, "Betsy's counts are coming in!"

When it finally happened I couldn't have been more excited if I had won the lottery.

The nurses told us that the first sign that counts were coming in would be an improvement in Betsy's mouth and throat sores. (Before counts, the sores can't get better because there are no white cells to heal them.)

Betsy's throat and mouth started to feel better a few days before the counts showed up on her blood test. Still, when the news came, it was a moment to remember. For me, it was similar to the times Betsy woke me up with the news she was pregnant, when I felt so proud, thankful, and overwhelmed to be greeted first thing in the morning by a miracle.

· · · · · · · · · · · · · · · · ·

CaringBridge Update: Saturday, September 10, 2005

In general, I'm not a big fan of being roused from a deep sleep at 5:30 a.m., but this morning was the exception. At 5:30 a nurse came into Betsy's room to tell her that she's starting to produce white blood cells! This is really big news—and a moment that we've been waiting for since her transplant.

I was awoken by the sound of the nurse excitedly telling Betsy that her blood showed a white cell count of 400. This is far below the 4,500 to 10,000 count that one normally has, but it's a huge step in the right direction, and it means her new stem cells have grafted into her bones and are starting to produce!

After the nurse left the room, I crawled out of bed and congratulated Betsy. We cracked open a fresh bottle of water and enjoyed a "water toast" of this incredible accomplishment. I am so proud of her.

This is one of those moments that make you stop and think about how far we've come and what a miracle we are witnessing. Those German stem cells have found their way across the ocean and into Betsy's bones. Now they're officially a part of Betsy and are starting to produce a brand new immune system for her. It's a mind-boggling journey.

The white count is a big step, but there's a lot more work to do, so now I ask you to concentrate on two things:

1. Please continue to send thoughts, prayers, and energy to those newly productive stem cells to keep them producing more and more blood cells.
2. Concentrate on those new white cells enjoying their new home inside of Betsy and working to heal her mouth and throat. This is the time when Betsy could start to develop graft-versus-host disease, a condition where Betsy's new white cells start to realize they're not in the body of a nineteen-year-old German and start attacking the foreign body that surrounds them, including Betsy's organs. A little graft-

versus-host disease can be fine, because often the white cells will attack any remnant cancer cells, but we don't want to have very much of this. We want those new white cells working their magic to bring Betsy relief instead.

We're now at day 17, meaning we've been in the hospital for twenty-four days.

· · · · · · · · · · · · · · · · ·

CaringBridge Update: Saturday, September 17, 2005

Over the past week we've received welcome news every morning upon receipt of Betsy's latest white blood cell counts. We saw the numbers move quickly...400...300 (a slight and not unexpected dip)...400...1,000...3,000...6,300! The high numbers prompted the doctors to stop giving her "growth factor," which helps spur cell production, to see if she can maintain the counts on her own. So far, so good. Her counts were 5,900 yesterday and 4,300 today. The progress with cell production is amazing, and we continue to be grateful for the donation of such hardworking stem cells!

One of the immediate effects of these lofty white counts is that Betsy is now free to leave her room for short walks as long as she wears a mask. It might not sound like such a bonus to be granted permission to walk around the halls of a hospital unit, but after being cooped up for a month in the room, simply passing through the doorway is a major relief.

Betsy and I have taken numerous "romantic strolls" around the BMT ward. It's actually pretty exciting. The nurses who have cared for Betsy get huge smiles on their faces and cheer her on when they see her walking around.

We are now at day 24. This is a critical time on two fronts: risk of infection and risk of graft–versus-host disease (GVHD).

First, while Betsy has a lot of white cells now, her immune system is far from normal. It will take up to a year before everything starts performing the way it should, so she is extremely vulnerable to infection.

Earlier this week Betsy ran a fever for a few days, and while this is not unexpected, it is always cause for concern and investigation. The fever is gone now, which is a great sign, but she does have some fluid in her lungs. To try to figure out what exactly is going on, they had to put a tube into her lungs today to draw out some fluid for analysis. Not a pleasant procedure, but necessary to help us stay on top of things. She did great, and we're hopeful that the tests will help us get rid of this issue quickly.

GVHD also starts to emerge with the production of Betsy's new white cells. So far there has been minimal evidence. Again, a little GVHD is good because it usually means the new cells are killing off any stray cancer cells still in her body. We just need to hope that the new white cells take a liking to the rest of Betsy and decide not to attack.

When you are sending thoughts and prayers, please concentrate on:

1. Helping Betsy fight off any infections.
2. Helping her new white cells feel comfortable in their new home so they'll only attack things that need attacking.

Betsy is starting to get antsy to go home, but at the same time we know we need to get on solid footing before then to avoid having to check back in at a later date. This is a hard time, because one day she'll feel good and the next day can be tough. Still, we are focused on how far she's come, and she is able to keep both her strength and her spirits up.

The girls are doing great. They have visited the hospital numerous times, which is always a treat. Julia finished her first full week of school, and she seems to love this new experience. She also talks with Betsy on the phone every night before bed so they can blow each other kisses through the phone. The girls have no idea how much strength they are giving to their parents through this fight.

· · · · · · · · · · · · · · · ·

It's hard to overstate the magnitude of the phrase, "Your counts are coming in." It's a remarkable moment, because it is the first sign that your body is responding to treatment. The chemo and radiation pre-transplant take you as close to death as possible, and the appearance of new white cells are the first indication that you are fighting your way back.

For Betsy, after a long and difficult stretch, that moment signaled an incredible turnaround where the momentum completely shifted to the side of progress.

She was able to once again get on the treadmill in her room, and we were able to go for our walks. To be honest, it was a little scary to take her out of her "cocoon" and walk around the unit the first time. But emotionally, it worked wonders for Betsy. While a mask hid most of her face, her eyes conveyed an enormous smile.

The walks also served to remind us of the community that we were now a part of, as we walked past room after room of patients fighting their own fights.

We didn't know many of the patients, but we could learn a lot from the drawings and messages on their whiteboards outside their rooms. Many families decorated the doors or wrote notes on whiteboards about what was going on inside. There was one boy who was a Green Bay Packers fan and would write his predictions for the Packers game that week (always a win) and the Vikings game as well (always a loss).

Many patients kept track of their days post-transplant on the door. Our hearts would sink seeing some of the numbers for patients who were in prolonged fights, "Day 110"…"Day 120." News on other doors displayed happier news, "My counts came in!" or, "Going home!!!"

On our walks we always made a point of walking by Vanessa's room to check on her progress. Along with updates, her board always carried a message from her parents, "So proud of Vanessa!"

Walking by arm in arm with Betsy, I understood. I felt the same way.

CHAPTER 16

. . . .

Stepping Out

. . . .

CaringBridge Update: **Monday, September 19, 2005**

The only thing you can really count on when going through a bone marrow transplant is that you can't predict anything. A good day can quickly turn into a tough day, and difficult times can suddenly yield a breakthrough. Luckily, yesterday was one of those significant leaps forward as Betsy took her first steps outside of the hospital in more than a month!

Yesterday morning, Betsy's white count was 7,300, meaning she's maintaining a very strong white count on her own. This prompted the doctor to decide that Betsy can take walks outside now, as long as she is wearing a mask. Considering that she has been battling fevers off and on for the last week as well as a very difficult cough, permission to go out into the world was unexpected, but welcome.

Betsy's mom brought Julia and Molly to the hospital, and the nurse temporarily disconnected Betsy from her IV tower for the first time since her radiation treatments ended. With Betsy enjoying her freedom from the tubes and pumps that have been her constant companions, we all ventured out of her room, down the all-too-familiar hallway of the BMT unit, into the elevator, through the lobby, and out into a beautiful, sunny day.

Julia and Molly were thrilled to have Mommy out walking with them. When Betsy asked Julia if she thought Mommy looked funny with her bald head and facemask, Julia said, "No…I think you look sweet."

We made our way to the courtyard of the hospital complex where there's a small playground. Betsy got to push Julia on the swing. We then wandered to the River Road and a small grassy area where we could sit and play with the girls. After about forty-five minutes, we made our way back to the hospital and toasted the occasion with chocolate milk.

It was amazing to see Betsy out and about after several days of feeling very weak, low energy, and feverish. She was obviously energized by the prospect of going outside, and seeing the girls brought extra spring to her step. When I told Julia how much Betsy had enjoyed seeing her and Molly, Julia said, "We're like medicine for her." It's true—and the medicine worked very well.

We're reaching the point where we start to hear rumblings about "going home." But before that happens, some significant work needs to be done. Her cell production appears to be maintaining itself and is sufficient for release, but she needs to start eating enough to sustain herself (which isn't easy when you're not feeling well and you haven't eaten anything of note in four weeks). She also needs to be free of fevers and infection before she can be discharged. We need to find out what's going on with her lungs and her sinuses to be sure she's in good shape for going home.

. . . .

After a transplant there are small but definite steps that need to be taken toward recovery and release. You can start to check them off your list and see how each milestone brings you closer to home.

- Chemo and radiation – DONE
- Transplant – DONE
- Counts come in – DONE
- Walk the halls – DONE
- Walk outside – DONE
- All clear of viruses and infection –
- Go home –

Obviously at this point we were feeling like we were in the home stretch, and that made Betsy's walk outside particularly exciting—and nerve racking.

I remember heading out for that walk with Betsy. As we arrived at the entrance to 4B, the BMT unit, my pulse quickened and I had to take a deep breath to steady myself. I hit the button and watched the double doors slowly open. Walking through, I thought about how the context of a situation can change the way you look at something, even something as simple as a pair of doors.

My first encounter with the doors to 4B came when we took our tour of the unit after Betsy's diagnosis. I felt a sense of dread walking through those doors, like I was entering a prison cell where we were going to be doing time.

Later, when we checked into 4B, the doors had changed. That entryway was no longer menacing. It was more mysterious. It was a passage to something unknown.

As the weeks passed, the doors slowly began to feel different, more comfortable, almost like a second home.

When the time came for Betsy to go *out* of those doors for the first time since her transplant, my perspective changed completely. Now the doors seemed like a protective barrier, a safe zone where the dangers of the outside world couldn't get to us.

As the doors slowly opened and we shuffled through, I held on tight to Betsy's arm, subconsciously doing what I could to protect her now that the doors were no longer there to do the job.

In a very strange way, that first walk gave me a sense of déjà vu. As we walked arm in arm, taking slow, deliberate steps, it almost felt like our wedding day.

I had to consciously slow down to equal Betsy's pace. We were both brimming with excitement and nerves, but we didn't speak. And while I'm sure it wasn't true, I felt like every eye was on us, watching us walk down the hall. Everyone was smiling and sharing our moment.

The wedding analogy of course falls apart quickly. Betsy's dress was replaced by a bathrobe. Her veil was now a facemask, her bouquet an IV stand, and her wedding hairdo was now a bald head.

Still, on this day, we shared the same sense of moving forward together, uncertain about what exactly the future holds, but confident great things lie ahead. Most important, just like on our wedding day, I couldn't have been more proud to be walking with Betsy at my side.

The number one benefit of having the transplant at a facility close to home was that Julia and Molly could visit whenever they were feeling healthy. If we had been forced to travel to a BMT facility, those visits would have been much more sporadic and complicated.

One of our friends in the unit, Bonnie, had traveled from San Francisco for her transplant. She also had two daughters, and her husband would fly them in for visits every couple of weeks. One time I remember they were scheduled to come, and at the last minute they got colds and had to cancel. I can't imagine the disappointment, and how hard it would be to have that much distance between you and your children when you're going through such a difficult time.

For Betsy, having the girls come in was a form of therapy. It's not an overstatement to say that Betsy lives for her daughters. She is a loving and devoted mother. Being a mom is the most important part of her life.

Julia and Molly were both at very fun and important ages when Betsy was diagnosed. In those early years, they learn every day. Their personalities are developing and they are growing fast. You don't want to miss a day.

Betsy's diagnosis forced her to miss a lot of these moments. She was in bed a lot from pain. She had to hand over many basic parenting duties to her mom. And the stress and worry of the situation made it difficult for her to give the girls the kind of time and attention she would normally devote to them.

When you add to that a long hospital stay in the BMT, you can see that time with the girls was a necessity. As Julia had put it earlier, it was Betsy's best medicine. So whenever the girls would visit to go for a walk or to read a story in bed with Betsy, I would often just sit back and take in the scene.

During that first walk outside, I could tell the girls understood the importance of the moment. Betsy's eyes again revealed the happiness and pride of her face behind that mask.

Betsy sat with the girls. She hugged them. If she ever needed a reminder of what she was fighting for, this was it. And the way the girls smiled and held her hand and laughed, it showed that time away doesn't change anything.

They were with their mommy, whom they love more than anything.

And this was a snapshot of what lay on the horizon. It was a chance to remind ourselves that we would get there, and that all would be well once again.

It wasn't long after Betsy's counts came in before thoughts of going home began to creep into our consciousness. We didn't talk about it much because we didn't want to get our hopes up, but each time we took a step forward, I knew it was on our minds.

One day, after a stretch when Betsy really seemed to be making strides, I met a woman who changed my perspective and my eagerness to get Betsy home.

Betsy had been taking regular walks, multiple times a day. She was getting some energy back. She was starting to get a little antsy to go home.

Betsy's counts were strong and everything was heading in the right direction. Other than a cough that crept up out of nowhere, Betsy appeared to be ready to go.

Around this time Betsy sent me to the kitchen to get her something to drink and some soup. As I waited for the soup to heat in the microwave, a woman came in for something.

I recognized her from numerous encounters in the hallways and the kitchen and said, "Hi." There were a lot of family members I knew by face in 4B, and a handful I knew by name, but I had never had a conversation with this woman before. From the look in her eyes that day, I knew she wanted to talk.

"How are things going?" I asked, (a normally clichéd greeting but one that actually has meaning when you ask someone on 4B).

"My daughter, Stephanie…she's having a hard time," said the woman, looking me in the eyes. "She's not going to make it."

My heart sank.

"What happened?" was all I could think of saying.

"She was doing great," said the woman. "She was at plus twenty-four and the doctors were talking about sending her home. Then she got a cough and it was a fungus in her lungs. They've been trying to stop it, but there's nothing they can do now."

The woman's eyes were full of tears, but the tears stayed there, welled up, frozen in a glassy expression.

"She's not going to make it," she said again. I almost got the feeling this was the first time she had said this out loud, and she said it again as if she was still coming to terms with the awful truth.

I muttered something about how sorry I was. I may have said it twice. I walked back to Betsy's room and paused for some deep breaths before going in.

I entered to the sound of Betsy coughing. We were around day 24. Betsy looked at me and smiled.

"The nurse just came in and said the doctors are thinking about a timeline to go home!" she said. "They dropped off a videotape about getting discharged that we're supposed to watch!"

I tried to convey excitement, but I felt fear and anxiety washing over me. I played the discharge tape and tried to watch, but the sound of Betsy coughing and the memory of the look on Stephanie's mom's face, which was burned on my brain, made it hard to pay attention.

I didn't tell Betsy about my conversation in the kitchen—and Betsy's cough did turn into one last major hurdle to face in 4B.

CHAPTER 17

. . . .

Steps Toward Home

One of the steps toward discharge is home health education—learning to take care of Betsy's catheter, including how to flush the line and change the dressing in a sanitary fashion and other details that will be needed once the nurses aren't around to take care of her.

Despite the fact that I had seen the nurses flush Betsy's line dozens of times, I was still a little nervous about doing it myself. The catheter is a direct line into Betsy's heart. If germs are introduced and the line becomes infected, the consequences can be disastrous.

I soon realized the reality of "line maintenance" is more about common sense than anything else.

- Use a lot of alcohol wipes.
- Don't touch any parts that will screw into the port.
- Only unclamp a line when you are actively running something through it, otherwise things are always clamped.

The most challenging task for me was getting all the air bubbles out of the syringe before injecting the saline (to flush the line) or heparin (to keep the line clear when it's not being used). I lived in fear of introducing an air bubble into Betsy's line and causing an embolism. The nurses taught me some tricks of the trade (like hitting the side of the syringe with a pen to dislodge the bubbles that stick to the side). After a while, even the air bubble elimination became routine.

But as Betsy's mom and I got comfortable with our roles, Betsy's discomfort was growing. Her cough had progressed to the point where it was an obvious concern. She would cough so hard she couldn't breathe, and from time to time an episode would get so bad she would gag. The drugs and antibiotics weren't helping. We needed to figure out what was going on.

The doctor ordered a bronchoscopy, a procedure in which a tiny camera and tube are sent down the patient's trachea into her lungs so they can shoot saline into the recesses and suction it back up to get samples of whatever is residing there. They take these samples to the lab and try to grow a virus, fungus, or bacteria so it can be identified and treated.

The day of the bronchoscopy, they wheeled in three carts' worth of equipment, followed by a team of people in gowns and masks.

They gave Betsy some drugs to relax her and knock her out just enough so they could do the procedure. A nurse told me the medication would keep her from remembering what was happening. I've learned that whenever they tell you that, something unpleasant is about to happen.

I met the doctors. One was older and was there to supervise and assist. The other was younger and obviously hadn't performed the procedure very many times. He didn't seem scared. To the contrary, he seemed a little too eager to get started. He shorthanded his explanation of the procedure to me, answered a couple questions, and said, "Okay, let's get started."

I asked if I could hold Betsy's hand while he worked, and he said there wasn't enough room around the bed, but if I wanted to sit so I could see the monitor, that would be fine. Instead, I took a seat behind the monitor where I could see Betsy and watch everyone work.

This was the first time I had to watch something being done to Betsy without being able to hold her hand or touch her in some way. From the epidurals during the birth of our daughters, through the chemo and the transplant, I was always able to sit by her and squeeze her hand. As I watched, I realized how much holding her hand was a comfort to me as much as it was to her. Being separated from her while this team of doctors and nurses worked made me feel helpless and scared.

A bronchoscopy is one of the more unpleasant procedures I've watched. The doctor holds a device that looks like a video game controller to direct the tube and camera down the throat and into the lungs.

The sights and sounds make it a chaotic event. Betsy was ordered to cough hard at certain times to clear the path for the tubes. Then she would be told *not* to cough. In her half-conscious state, obeying orders like this was difficult. I wanted to be next to her, coaching her and helping her, but all I could do was watch.

There was a constant suction sound as they worked to clear mucus from her throat, and later to pull the water saline in after flushing it through her lungs. They had to hit multiple locations in each lung. It felt like it took an awfully long time.

At various times Betsy sounded like she was choking—not just gagging—choking. Sometimes the nurse would turn to me and say, "She's okay...don't worry...she won't remember any of this."

Again, that assurance didn't make me feel better. And it turned out they were wrong. To this day the word "bronchoscopy" sends a chill through Betsy.

When the procedure was finally over, everyone packed up to go. They had what they needed, and as unpleasant as the bronchoscopy was, it did the trick. Within days they identified an issue in her lungs and started an intense treatment that finally helped us get home.

. . . .

CaringBridge Update: Wednesday, September 21, 2005

Well, after an uplifting weekend, we find ourselves once again engaged in a fight. Betsy has been battling a bad cough and congestion for a while now, and yesterday they figured out the cause. Betsy has a virus—the influenza A virus—so now we need to concentrate our thoughts and prayers to knock it out of her system.

For the past week or so, even during the initial discussions about going home, Betsy and I both knew that going home wasn't going to be an option until we figured out and cured the issue with her lungs. So when we were informed that they had diagnosed the problem as this influenza virus, we were actually a little relieved. Once we know what the problem is, we can concentrate on beating it.

There are three types of infections to worry about: viral, bacterial, and fungal. Of these three, it's my understanding that fungal is usually the worst. We have more ways to treat the viral and bacterial infections. It was a relief to see that as soon as the doctors figured out the problem, they had a protocol ready to get rid of it.

Betsy is receiving special antibiotics through her catheter during the day and a very powerful drug called ribavirin at night. This drug is administered through a mask that she has to wear while she sleeps.

Because of the virus and the treatment, I can't go into the room now without wearing a gown, mask, and gloves to avoid spreading the virus to other patients. I also can't sleep in the room while she's receiving the ribavirin unless I wear a heavy mask, gown, and gloves. For this reason I'm sleeping at home now until her treatment is done.

The ribavirin treatments will go on for five nights. The girls can't visit her during this time either, so it's going to be a tough stretch, but as usual Betsy is rising to the challenge. After just one night of treatment I could see a noticeable difference. She looks great and her cough is a little better. I'm convinced that she's going to knock this virus out quickly, breaking through this final barricade to clear the path for her return home.

Your thoughts, support, and prayers play a significant role in Betsy's recovery, so we ask that right now you concentrate all of your efforts on this virus, helping her eliminate it from her system.

· · · · · · · · · · · · · · · · ·

Because Betsy's mom was living with us, I had the luxury of staying at the hospital with Betsy throughout her transplant and recovery. I would usually go home once a day to spend some time with the girls, to eat dinner with them or read stories and put them to bed. I would also take a moment to get cleaned up. Other than that I was at 4B.

And while luxury might not be the best word to describe sleeping in a hospital room for six weeks in a row, it was definitely beneficial to be there. I got to know the nurses and appreciated the way they always took time to explain things to me and answer questions. I never missed a visit from the doctors, so I always knew where things stood and I could get my questions and concerns addressed.

In the really difficult times, it was especially important to always know what was going on. When Betsy was having trouble breathing and the oxygen meter alarm would sound, I could hop out of bed and check on Betsy. When she would wake up in the middle of the night hallucinating, I could hold her hand and calm her down. She may not have always been aware that I was there, but I believe it helped her. I know it helped me.

When the doctors started treatment for the influenza A virus, this "luxury" was taken away. All of a sudden I wasn't allowed to sleep in the room with Betsy anymore.

The nurses explained that ribavirin is a very potent drug that is inhaled overnight. It actually ends up going into the air and leaves a slight film of dust around the room by morning. So not only was I not allowed to sleep in the room, I couldn't even enter without putting on a special gown, gloves, and a mask.

I remember the strange feeling of kissing Betsy goodnight and leaving her the first night of the treatment. I'd be lying to say I wasn't looking forward to sleeping in my bed at home, but I also felt on edge. Other than her sessions in the radiation room, this was the first time I wasn't able to be at her side.

I got home that night and kissed the girls while they were sleeping. I crawled into our bed and felt the unwelcome void of not having Betsy next to me. My mind wandered. I couldn't sleep.

For some reason, lying in our room made my thoughts race more than lying on the mattress in the hospital. I found myself reflecting on the last weeks and months and wondering about the weeks and months ahead. I thought about Betsy alone in her room, breathing in this potent medicine that would hopefully clear her lungs.

I put on a movie. It took my mind off of things. I finally fell asleep.

For the next five days, while the ribavirin treatments continued, this became my routine. The *Star Wars* trilogy and *Indiana Jones* became my nightly dose of escapism to help me get to sleep. In the morning, I would kiss the girls goodbye and head back to the hospital. I put on the gown, gloves, and mask, and was back in the strange security of 4B.

. . . .

CaringBridge Update: Thursday, September 29, 2005

Today was a big day. Six weeks after checking into the hospital, and five weeks after her transplant, Betsy is HOME! We said goodbye to the hospital at around 2:00 this afternoon, marking the end of a major part of this journey and the beginning of the next stage of recovery.

The doctors had been talking about sending Betsy home since Monday, but things kept getting delayed to be sure she was getting enough nutrition, was able to take her pills, and was progressing after the virus treatment. To be honest, I think we were all a little worried about Betsy getting discharged too early, so each delay was more of a relief than a disappointment.

We actually moved out of the bone marrow transplant unit at the end of last week. They needed to open up a room for a new patient and decided Betsy was the most ready to move, so they sent us to a different oncology unit.

After more than a month in the BMT, it was surprisingly sad to leave. We had a great experience with the nurses, aides, physician's assistants, and doctors. You get to know everyone pretty well spending that much time together, and we felt lucky to have such wonderful, caring people around us. They were sad to see Betsy go as well. Through some very difficult times, Betsy was always a kind and gracious patient. I had more than one nurse tell me how much everyone enjoyed having her around.

The unit they moved us to was very different. Because it wasn't a BMT unit we felt more exposed. There were more people in the halls and more open doors to patients' rooms. It also was a much smaller room, with no Internet access, no VCR—we couldn't hook up the DVD player. It was probably a good transition to get us ready to go home.

By the end of the day yesterday, it was apparent that today would be the day. This morning, the doctors looked Betsy over one more time, checked her blood counts, and wrote up the discharge orders. We packed up her room. I went to the checkout pharmacy to pick up a startlingly heavy bag of drugs, and we drove home.

Leaving the security of the hospital was scary, but our anxiety faded immediately when we saw the smiles on Julia and Molly's faces. Mommy was home! The girls have been so strong throughout Betsy's hospital stay, but six weeks is a long time. I could have sat and watched the reunion for hours—all three of them frolicking on the bed—Julia jumping and shouting, "I'm really excited! I'm really excited!" and Molly crawling back and forth across Betsy's lap, diving into Mommy's arms with a look of complete joy.

Betsy still doesn't feel good, and she probably won't feel good for at least a few more months. So now, as we prepare for the next stage of this fight, we need to keep our guard up. Please focus your thoughts and prayers to help Betsy:

- Avoid infection. She is still extremely vulnerable to illness.
- Avoid significant graft-versus-host disease (GVHD).

We will be going into the clinic every day for the foreseeable future for checkups, blood tests, and transfusions. And while it will be nice for Betsy to be around her family and to sleep in her own bed, things will continue to be far from normal. We still have a lot of restrictions including:

- No flowers or plants in the house due to risk of infection, and
- No visitors other than immediate family.

It's not uncommon for BMT patients to have to check back into the hospital for infections or severe GVHD. We want to take every precaution to avoid that if at all possible.

There was something surreal about the drive home today. The last time Betsy and I were in the car together, it was the night after she checked in and got her catheter installed. We were having one last dinner out before she started chemo. Today, I couldn't help but think about how far we've come.

. . . .

CHAPTER 18

. . . .

Staying on Guard

When you arrive home post-transplant, you are always on edge. Not only because of the fact that someone you love is in such a weakened state, or that there is so much to keep track of (pills, appointments, flushing the catheter, etc.), but also because of the primary fear—infection. Every cough or sniffle makes you sit up and take notice. A fever requires an immediate call to the hospital.

To contact the BMT after hours we had to call the main hospital number and ask to speak to the BMT fellow on call. I learned to be clear and say "bone marrow transplant fellow" to avoid the confusion that once left me explaining Betsy's GVHD symptoms to a very confused ear, nose, and throat (ENT, not BMT) physician.

The BMT fellow runs through a series of questions:

- How many days is Betsy post-transplant?
- What type of cancer?
- What medications is she taking?
- What type of catheter does she have?
- What's her temperature?

Sometimes the fellow was someone we knew from the hospital. Sometimes not. Either way, it was comforting to talk with someone who really understood the post-transplant risks. And if Betsy's temperature was more than 101 degrees, the chances were good we'd be sent to the emergency room.

On those occasions, having Betsy's mom living with us was a god-

Family photo taken a few months before Betsy's diagnosis. Blissfully unaware that Betsy had cancer.

A happy homecoming. Betsy and the girls reunited after a six-week hospital stay. Unfortunately, it was a brief return before another, longer, hospital stay.

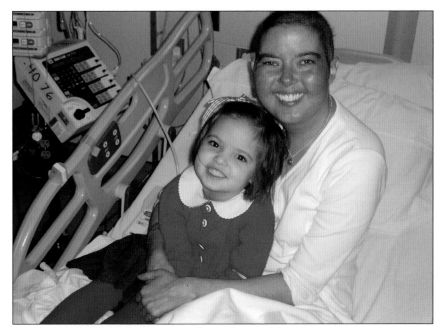

Visits from Julia and Molly brought joy to the hospital room.

Participation in fundraising events like the Leukemia & Lymphoma Society's Light the Night Walk allowed us to give back to organizations that helped us along the way.

Betsy's first meeting with Tobias, the man who saved her life.

A trip of a lifetime. Visiting Germany for the wedding of Betsy's stem cell donor.

Betsy and Tobias dancing on his wedding night, and our tenth anniversary.

A celebration five years in the making. Betsy is finally considered "cured" of cancer.

send. Rather than packing up the girls for a midnight trip to the ER, or having to wake someone up to come over and babysit, we could just head out to the car and go.

The BMT fellow would call the ER to alert them we were coming and to give instructions about our care. Usually this meant we didn't have to wait too long to be seen. Still, when you have a severely compromised immune system, sitting in an ER waiting room at midnight is probably the last place you want to be.

Usually the visit involved checking Betsy's blood counts, and perhaps starting her on an antibiotic. The doctors always seemed to take extra care with Betsy, knowing her history. We would head home again in the middle of the night with at least some peace of mind that we had been seen and checked out, but we knew we'd have to be back at the BMT clinic in the morning to look for more answers. In the immediate post-transplant world, vigilance is the key. Even the smallest symptom had to be addressed to keep Betsy on the right path.

. . . .

CaringBridge Update: Thursday, October 6, 2005

Over the last week, since Betsy came home, we have received welcome reminders about how lucky we are and how far we've come, and a less welcome reminder of much work we still have to do. It's on this second point that we ask you to once again send out your strongest thoughts and prayers for healing.

Betsy has been dealing with a cough for a few weeks now. When we found the influenza virus in her lungs, we were hopeful that a solution was at hand and she would soon be breathing easier. While the ribavirin treatment brought some improvement and allowed Betsy to get cleared to come home, the cough has persisted. Today, a new CT scan showed that some of the spots in her lungs have improved, but there are some new spots that need attention.

These spots could be caused by the same influenza virus or they could be the result of a bacterial or fungal infection. We need to figure out the cause quickly so Betsy can get on a course of treatment for a cure.

In an attempt to determine exactly what's going on in her lungs, Betsy is going in tomorrow morning for another bronchoscopy. It's a very unpleasant procedure, and one we hoped Betsy would not have to deal with again, but we know that it's a necessary step and we want to do everything possible to knock this infection out of her system.

Once they've done the bronchoscopy, they'll start Betsy on a new antifungal medication and an antibacterial medication to hopefully start fighting whatever is in her lungs immediately. Then, when we get the results back, we can adjust her medication. Uncertainty is never easy, but we're hopeful that this next step will clarify what we're dealing with so we can move forward.

The other development in recent days is that we've seen the emergence of some graft-versus-host disease (GVHD) in the form of a rash. This is not at all unexpected. As I have mentioned before, a little GVHD can actually be good, because if there are any cancer cells left in Betsy's body, her new immune system is probably attacking them. The doctors are monitoring the GVHD to make sure it doesn't attack Betsy's organs, but so far, it's a very manageable case.

Given the current medical issues, we ask that you concentrate all your efforts again on two goals:

1. We need to get rid of any and all infections in Betsy's lungs.
2. We need to stop the spread of the GVHD and keep it at an easily manageable level.

Despite the new challenges, the last week has been a welcome change. Watching Betsy read to the girls, getting a chance to have meals together as a family, and enjoying a walk through the neighborhood are all simple pleasures, but they have taken on new meaning. Betsy's energy level is very low, so she can't be as active as I know she'd like to be, but her presence alone brings an energy and joy to the house that was sorely missed.

We did receive some positive news on the medical front a few days ago. The results from a DNA test on Betsy's blood came back showing a 100 percent DNA match with her bone marrow donor. This means that her new cells have grafted very well and have completely replaced her old blood with new blood. It's a very positive sign in terms of avoiding any issues with relapse in the future.

It can be a little discouraging when these new issues arise. But when I see Molly walking toward Betsy with outstretched arms, smiling and saying, "Mama," over and over again, or when I see Betsy and Julia talking excitedly about what Julia did at school, I can't help but think about how far we've come just to get these moments back. Betsy has been fighting so hard and has never wavered in her resolve to do whatever we have to do to knock this CML out of her system for good. These moments in time remind us of the stakes that we are playing for and rejuvenate us for the next battle, which I have no doubt we will win.

. . . .

CaringBridge Update: Friday, October 14, 2005

When Betsy was first diagnosed, we received some very good advice: Don't look too far down the road. Try to concentrate on each day and tackle the challenge in front of you.

As we continue in this recovery, we have learned another lesson: When you're evaluating your progress, be sure to look at the big picture. Progress might seem slow on some days, but remember how many huge steps forward you've taken to get to this point.

Both of these lessons are very much in play right now, as Betsy fights issues in her lungs, deals with graft-versus-host disease, and works to get enough nutrition into her body to stay healthy.

As we mentioned in the last update, Betsy has had a persistent cough and had to have a bronchoscopy to try to figure out what was going on in her lungs. A few days ago the doctors identified *two* infections in her lungs: one bacterial and one fungal.

Learning that Betsy is battling two new infections was a little disconcerting because she is still extremely vulnerable, and fungal infections in particular can be tough to cure. On the positive side, we now know what we're dealing with and the doctors can take steps to knock this stuff out. Betsy has started to receive major doses of antibiotics every day during her clinic visits, and we're optimistic we'll finally get her lungs cleared out so we can put this challenge in the rearview mirror.

On the second front, Betsy's GVHD has progressed but is still well under control. So far it has only presented as a rash. She is taking medicine now to prevent it from attacking her organs.

The third concern we're facing is getting Betsy enough nutrition to maintain her health. Over the last week it has become more difficult for Betsy to eat and her nausea has increased. While she's been able to eat soups, popsicles, and the occasional chocolate malt, she has lost a lot of weight. To try to reverse that trend Betsy is going to start getting nutrition through her catheter again, just as she did in the hospital when she couldn't eat.

A home health care provider stopped by last night to teach Betsy's mom and me about hooking up the feeding tubes to run overnight. These large bags of syrup-like protein and thick white lipids may not seem very appetizing, but they should give Betsy a much-needed boost, helping her to feel better and more energetic. While it may feel like a setback to go back onto a feeding tube, we see it as a step forward. It will help her over the current hurdle and give her strength to forge ahead.

In light of the recent developments, we ask you to concentrate your thoughts and prayers on helping us beat the infections in Betsy's lungs. Now that we know there are two infections, please visualize both of them getting wiped out by the waves of antibiotics entering her system.

The last few days have been a challenge because Betsy simply doesn't feel good. She gets very tired and has spent a lot of time resting on the couch or in bed. This is not necessarily bad. Her body is engaged in a tough battle, so it's important to rest. I just know that it's frustrating for her to not be up and about, playing with the girls and participating the way she'd like to be.

We reached another milestone worth noting yesterday as we crossed off day 50 from the post-transplant calendar. In a way it seems like it's been a lot longer than fifty days since those over-achieving German stem cells were introduced into Betsy's body. At the same time, day 50 presents a nice chance to look back on how far Betsy has come. In less than two months she has kicked the cancer cells out of her body and started up an entirely new immune system. Her stem cells are producing good quantities of red cells, white cells, and platelets. And she's been able to return home to her family where, even in her weakened state, she lifts the spirits of everyone around her.

. . . .

CaringBridge Update: Tuesday, October 25, 2005

Over the last week, things have definitely moved in a positive direction. Betsy's energy level has picked up, she's been able to start eating again, and the graft-versus-host disease appears to be more under control.

I always feel like I can tell immediately each day if Betsy is trending up or down just by the look in her eyes. Ten days ago, she was struggling. Betsy's energy level was low and it was hard for her to get out of bed. Then, about five days ago, she woke up and the sparkle was back in her eyes. The combination of the nutrition she's getting through her catheter and the medication for the GVHD gave her some energy and an appetite. It's amazing how quickly things can change.

The other major concern we've been dealing with is the infection in Betsy's lungs. On Saturday the doctor informed us that they were able to identify the specific fungus that we're dealing with. It's called *Beauveria*.

All we know about *Beauveria* is that it's very rare to be found in humans. It is a soil-based fungus and is sometimes used as a pesticide, so if you're an aphid, a weevil, a mealybug, or a similar type of pest, you don't want to have anything to do with *Beauveria*. The doctors assured us that it's not necessarily bad to have a rare fungus, and that the medicine she's receiving is very good at fighting many types of fungal infections.

The good news is that Betsy's symptoms are getting better. A new CT scan of her lungs today showed significant improvement. So while the specialists are going to continue looking at this *Beauveria* fungus to make sure we're doing everything we can, all indications are that the treatment is knocking the fungus out of her system.

The day-to-day routine for Betsy right now consists of waking up, taking a laundry list of medications, and going off to the BMT clinic, where she spends anywhere from three to five hours getting her antifungal medication and any blood or nutritional infusions that she might need. When she returns home she'll try to eat and rest. At night she takes more medications and we hook up her bag of nutrition to her catheter to run overnight.

While the daily schedule might seem monotonous, every single step is an important part of this fight. Every day we cross off on the calendar is a victory. And every day I am amazed by Betsy's determination and her ability to focus on the long-term goal.

A few nights ago, I was reading to Julia in bed when she turned to me and said, "Daddy, do you remember when Momma had cancer?" I smiled at her use of the past tense in reference to the disease and said, "Yes, and she's still working hard to fight it." Julia smiled and said, "She's saying, 'Shoo…shoo, cancer…shoo, shoo, shoo,'" and she waved her hands in a dismissing motion. I believe that Julia was right, and that day 100 will reveal Betsy's overwhelming victory over CML.

. . . .

CHAPTER 19

. . . .

Back to the BMT

Journal Entry – November 5, 2005

I got a call at work today from Betsy's mom to tell me that a decision had been made: Betsy is being readmitted to the hospital. I wasn't surprised.

For the last week it has been obvious that her GVHD was getting worse. Pain in Betsy's gut was getting extreme. She isn't sleeping well and she spends most of her time in bed or in the bathroom.

Betsy's condition is taking both a physical and mental toll. Obviously the pain from the GVHD is difficult to endure. But I know it's also hard for Betsy to feel so bad around the girls. She can't be as engaged with them as she would like to be and she loses her patience quickly, which is not like her at all. It's subtle. The girls may not really notice much, but I know Betsy is aware of it and she feels bad about it.

Two nights ago Susan was hooking up Betsy's total parenteral nutrition (TPN) (the nutrition she receives through her catheter) and Julia went in to watch. Julia watches a lot of the procedures. She has a genuine curiosity about how her mom is being treated.

On this particular night, Julia was coughing, so Betsy and Susan told her to leave. She went downstairs to look for me, but I was out walking the dog, and Julia started to cry. This woke up Molly and things got worse.

I came back in the house to hear a chorus of screams and wails. I ran upstairs, calmed Julia a little, got Molly back to sleep, and went back to talk to Julia about what was wrong.

"Mama and Nana told me to get out!" she said.

I asked if she understood why.

"Because I was coughing," she said.

"And do you know why you can't be in there when you're coughing?"

Julia looked at me with a serious expression, paused, and said, "It's just hard when someone has cancer that you really love."

She was right. All I could do was give her a hug. There was nothing else to say.

. . . .

CaringBridge Update: Saturday, November 5, 2005

Once again the cyclical nature of this fight against CML has presented a new challenge. So today we had to check Betsy back into the hospital, where she will get treatment for a bad case of graft-versus-host disease.

The GVHD in her gastrointestinal (GI) tract has had Betsy in a downward spiral—it has been preventing her body from properly absorbing her medication, which in turn makes her GVHD worse. We needed to do something to break this cycle, and today it was decided the best way to do that was to check back into the hospital where all the medicine can be administered through Betsy's catheter.

We were fortunate that a room opened up on 4B, the bone marrow transplant unit. It made Betsy feel much more comfortable to go back to a unit that she is familiar with and to see all the nurses and aides she got to know so well during her transplant. She's actually in the room next door to where she received her new stem cells.

We checked in to the hospital tonight and started to get settled into her room. The doctor explained the course of action and advised us to expect about a week-long stay this time. I know it was hard for Betsy to pack her bags and say goodbye to the girls for another hospital stay. At the same time, we both know this is the right thing to do. Betsy was extremely uncomfortable and was obviously getting worse. This treatment should provide relief and help her get past the GVHD so she can move ahead with a full recovery.

Having Betsy home, even in her weakened condition, has been wonderful. It was so nice just to see the joy on Betsy's face watching the girls model their Halloween costumes (Julia was a ballerina, Molly a ladybug). But our goal in this battle is a cure, and we look forward to the time when Betsy can fully participate in activities once again.

As we deal with the GVHD, we once again ask for your help. Please concentrate your thoughts and prayers on getting rid of the GVHD so Betsy can come home again. At the same time, continue your prayers for the complete elimination of the infections in Betsy's lungs. Her lungs are much better, but we need to be sure the fungal infections completely disappear.

Cancer is a terrible disease. Since Betsy's diagnosis I have become aware of so many people who have faced their own challenges. In fact, a good friend of ours is heading back to the hospital this week for a second round of treatment against his cancer, a fight that we hope and pray he will win.

As difficult as the fight is, though, cancer can't diminish the human spirit. Betsy remains an inspiration to me, handling her move back to the hospital with typical courage and grace. Now we have our sights set on beating the GVHD, another happy reunion when she comes home again, and continued progress toward a resounding defeat of this terrible disease.

* * * * * * * * * * * * * * * * *

Journal Entry – November 6, 2005

Checking back into 4B brought mixed emotions. I know that being readmitted is fairly common, but I had convinced myself that we would only be back to 4B to visit.

When we walked in as patients, I was a little discouraged, and when I saw some of the family members I knew from before, I felt this strange need to explain…"It's just for GVHD…she's really doing fine."

I didn't say anything, but I wanted to avoid the perception that we were in that "group," the patients who have to come back, who weren't making it on the outside.

The disappointment about being back was more than out-weighed, however, by a sense of relief. It was good to know Betsy was back under such watchful care. She was in a lot of pain, and the GVHD was getting worse and worse. As they checked her in and the doctor talked us through the treatment plan, I thought, "This is the place to be. This is where she *needs* to be right now."

Serious illness changes your perspective about everything—work, family, friendship, love—and it also changes your perspective about hardship and pain.

Before Betsy was diagnosed with cancer, the thought of even one night in the hospital was scary. Now, learning Betsy will be in for a week feels manageable and is actually a little comforting. Even saying goodbye to the girls was less traumatic because we have more of a big-picture view. This week will help us get back to the girls in a better, stronger state.

We slipped back into a 4B comfort zone fairly quickly. The routine is the same. The nurses are the same. It *almost* seems like we never left.

They have Betsy on some strong pain relievers and she's comfortable now, but we're back in another haze. And even though I know the drugs are helping her, I have to say it tears me up to see her back in this state.

Betsy sleeps all the time and is having strange dreams. The loud snoring is back, and even when Betsy is awake, she's on the edge of consciousness. She goes in and out of conversations unpredictably, and I have to talk her through taking her pills to prevent her from falling asleep in the middle of the process.

It's always hard to see her like this, but it might be harder this time because she was doing so well a week ago. It seems like such a regression. I know it is drug-induced, but it's frightening. Every time she comes out of one of these phases I pray I'll never see it again.

Betsy has been undergoing a number of different treatments for her GVHD. She's also getting treated for the side effects of the treatments. Part of this involves getting regular shots of insulin in her stomach. Betsy never bats an eye for any of the needle sticks or procedures. Even in this weakened state, she is so strong. I am amazed.

So far we haven't seen much progress in stopping the GVHD, so tonight they're going to start Betsy on a third drug. From what I've gathered, three is all they have.

This drug is supposed to be pretty powerful, so it should help, but I don't like being on any sort of a path where options are running out. I don't know what the implications would be if this drug doesn't work. I don't want to know. Right now I'm just focused on progress…breaking this cycle and getting Betsy back. I feel like this is a big hurdle, a push to the top of an incline, and when we get there we'll see a long horizon stretched out, waiting for us to move ahead.

Right now they're about to start an antithymocyte globulin (ATG), Atgam. It's similar to a blood product, and it comes from a horse. It suppresses the T-cells (the attack cells) in Betsy's blood, which will hopefully stop the GVHD in its tracks. I get the impression it is a powerful treatment. Hopefully the GVHD is about to face its last stand.

Journal Entry – November 8, 2005

I don't usually get mad about this whole situation…the CML…because it seems like an unproductive way of looking at things. Who am I mad at? What good would it do to walk around angry? We have no choice in this matter but to fight, and I believe positivity gets us further. Still, I have to say, anger has crept up on me more and more in recent days, ever since Betsy was readmitted.

I look at her lying in bed, sedated from painkillers, fighting so hard…and I can't help but be mad.

She has worked so hard, fought so hard, and come so far, and here we are back in 4B with the same pumps ticking away the hours, the same state of semi-consciousness that made us so scared a couple months ago, and the same prospect of a major battle ahead.

It's not fair that someone who has fought so bravely and has met her challenges with such strength should be back here, dealing with yet another uphill climb.

Right now we're in one of the really difficult phases. Betsy is not feeling well enough to take an active role in figuring out what is going on. She's sleeping so much it's hard to measure if she is getting better or worse.

We're in a haze right now, and without any way of knowing where we're headed, it's easy to let your mind race.

I need a sign.

I need a few signs.

I need to know the GVHD is responding.

I need to know her infections are clearing up.

I need to see the spark in her eyes.

I need to see her sense of humor returning.

I need to talk with her, to have a conversation about anything, just as long as she's engaged and involved.

I need her to move her hands and arms at a normal pace with normal dexterity rather than in the slow, overly deliberate fashion that she uses now.

I need her to breathe at a normal pace, without the long, drug-induced gaps between breaths that she gets now.

I'm not asking to snap my fingers for a full recovery. I just want a sign…progress…momentum…some relief.

I want something that will let her know we're getting there, and if she can just fight a little longer we're going to turn the corner and we'll be able to see the horizon. But right now all we can see is the incline, and I know how hard it has been just to get to this point.

So sometimes I get mad that she has no choice but to take these slow, painful, scary steps ahead up the hill, with no sign of the finish line. And I pray that rest, relief, and reward are just around the bend.

Journal Entry – November 9, 2005

Tonight I got home from work and sat down at the dinner table with the girls for a little quality time before heading to the hospital. Betsy called my cell phone to ask me a question. I asked Julia if she wanted to talk to Mommy.

Julia grabbed the phone and said, with no prompting, "Momma, you're so brave and so strong, you can do it!" She was pounding her hand on the table as she spoke. I watched in amazement, tears welling in my eyes.

After Betsy said something in response, Julia continued her cheer, "You go, Momma, go! You can do it! You're so strong! You're going to knock that cancer out of your body!"

Julia is so amazing to me. I am so proud of her. I know that cheer had to give Betsy a rush of energy.

Julia and Molly have no idea how much strength they give us.

Despite the fact that Betsy was back in familiar surroundings, being cared for by the same team, her second hospital stay was in many ways very different from her first.

During the transplant we had a road map to follow. We knew the different stages of treatment. We could anticipate the difficult stretches and prepare for them, even though sometimes they were tougher than we thought they would be. Betsy's progress was measurable—waiting for her counts to come in, tracking the white cell numbers—moving forward to get to the point where she could go home.

When Betsy returned to the hospital, we had no road map. There's no way to measure the progress, or to even know if the treatment is working. We had no timetable for when Betsy would get to come home. We went into it thinking she would be home in less than a week. We were very wrong.

Betsy's doctors had to get creative to treat Betsy during this time. It's not that they hadn't seen this kind of GVHD before, it's just that there isn't a set regimen to handle it. I could tell they were trying everything they could think of. I was glad to know how much brain power was going into Betsy's treatment plan. At the same time, it also made me feel a little desperate.

I was told the greatest hope for relief from the GVHD is ATG. This is a powerful treatment where they infuse a blood product derived from horses (or in some cases, pigs or rabbits) to try to suppress the T-cells that are causing the graft-versus-host disease. It's mind-boggling to think of all the science that we benefitted from throughout Betsy's journey. The idea that horse-blood products could save Betsy was difficult to wrap my brain around.

We were told it can sometimes take weeks to know if ATG is working. Still, we were hopeful this procedure would provide just the help we needed to start making strides forward.

Unfortunately, the wait was difficult. Betsy had day after day of pain, discomfort, and uncertainty. I was reduced once again to an observer, offering support however I could, but with the sad realization that no matter how much I wanted to, I couldn't make everything better.

After about a week, the doctors started to get concerned about the fact that we weren't seeing much progress. They decided to administer another ATG treatment (this one was a pig-blood product) in an effort to get things moving in the right direction.

The treatments Betsy was getting expanded. At one point they started administering injections of insulin into Betsy's stomach twice a day to try to counteract some of the side effects of treatments she was receiving. The injections were painful, but Betsy never complained.

That's not to say Betsy was breezing through this stage. The combination of pain, uncertainty, and an extended hospital stay well beyond what we anticipated was a lot to handle. One day it became too much, and Betsy broke down in tears. It was then that one of the worst moments we experienced in the hospital occurred.

There was a new doctor assigned to 4B for a stretch (everyone in the practice rotates through assignments on the unit). This was a doctor we didn't know very well, but she seemed nice, and we had a lot of confidence in that team.

On this day, she walked into Betsy's room with a sad, almost somber look on her face. I was sitting next to Betsy's bed holding her hand and trying to console her through one of her rare down moments. We looked up at the doctor expectantly, and we were both taken aback by the serious look on her face.

She took a deep breath, and reached out and grabbed Betsy's hand. She looked at Betsy and at me and paused again, looking as if she didn't know how to begin to say what she had to say.

My heart started to race. I knew Betsy's case was challenging and I had been told by doctors a couple of times that they had "one more thing they could try." I squeezed Betsy's hand and thought to myself, "She's about to tell me there's nothing more they can do."

I wasn't alone in this thought. Betsy squeezed my hand back and started crying again. We stared up at the doctor and braced ourselves.

"I understand you've been sad today," was how the doctor started.

"Ummm...yes...that's true," I thought to myself. "What does that have to do with her news."

The doctor continued, "Is there something wrong or something we can do?"

Huh?

"It's okay to be sad," she said, "but you have to try to keep strong for your family and your children."

And that was it.

I breathed out a sigh of relief, followed immediately by a moment of disbelief. Did the doctor realize how her attempt to reassure Betsy came off to us? Was she really trying to give Betsy a "be strong for your family" pep talk just because Betsy was having one down day during a particularly difficult stretch?

In the end I let it all go. I know the doctor was trying to be helpful, she just happened to hit us at a particularly vulnerable moment and her delivery of this message was a little off-key.

We had many more dealings with this doctor and she proved to be a very good caregiver. It's unfortunate that to this day I equate her with the one moment of Betsy's fight where I actually thought we were going to be defeated.

Fortunately, soon after this incident we started to see some signs that the ATG was working.

In an effort to speed up the process, and to allow her GI tract to heal from the GVHD, Betsy was told to not consume anything other than sips of water. No broth. No Jell-O. No food of any kind. This was particularly hard because Betsy was feeling okay and was finally starting to crave food. As a surrogate to take the place of eating, she started a project in her room—organizing her recipe books into binders. It was her way of living vicariously through the recipes and we anticipated the moment when she would be able to enjoy those dishes again.

When Betsy first checked back into the hospital, we all expected it would be a short stay. We didn't bring everything back with us. We didn't hang the pictures of the girls in the room. It was a slow adjustment to the realization that this was going to be another lengthy stay.

As the weeks passed, we marked Thanksgiving on the calendar, hoping to have her home by then. That didn't turn out to be the case. Instead, her doctors allowed her to be unhooked from her monitors to go home for a few hours of Thanksgiving family time. It was a fun surprise for the girls, and one that brought tears to my eyes, but it was a small consolation for not having her home for good. It was a less than ideal Thanksgiving, but never in our lives had we better understood what the day is really about.

. . . .

CaringBridge Update: Sunday, December 4, 2005

Today officially marks day 100 post-transplant.

When we were first learning about the bone marrow transplant timeline and the "day 100" milestone, I have to admit we had a different scenario in mind than the one we have in front of us today. I think we had it in our minds that Betsy would be home and feeling stronger by this time, not in the hospital facing further GVHD treatment.

We always knew there was nothing "magical" about day 100. It's simply a time when the doctors run a lot of tests to figure out where things stand. Still, despite the fact that Betsy remains in the hospital, we celebrate day 100 for what it is, a chance to reflect on what has been a remarkable journey thus far, and to give thanks for all of the support that has led us to this point.

Betsy's GI tract is still being hit by a serious case of graft-versus-host disease. We saw some improvement after the first round of ATG treatment, to the point where Betsy was allowed to consume some clear liquids, but things stalled over the last week, so she's back to not consuming anything. The doctors have started her on a second round of ATG. The feeling is that the first dose helped her part way down the road to recovery, so this second dose may be the trick to get her the rest of the way.

Day 100 is a milepost for learning how things are progressing with the transplant. It is marked by a flurry of tests, with the most notable being a bone marrow biopsy, which Betsy had on Thursday. This test will let us know what's going on in Betsy's marrow, and whether or not there is any hint of the CML left in her body. With the amount of GVHD she's had, we're hopeful Betsy's new stem cells have eliminated every last cancer cell. We'll get preliminary results from the biopsy this week.

As I mentioned in the last update, this hospital stay has been difficult emotionally and physically. GVHD can be tough to get rid of, and it can be very uncomfortable. At the same time, the treatments are intense, leaving Betsy extremely tired much of the day.

Emotionally, this is a tough time, primarily because one hundred days of fighting takes a toll. This is a twenty-four-hour-a-day battle, and Betsy can't take a day off to relax. After this much time, the aspects that are the hardest—separating from Molly and Julia, being away from home, missing her friends—all start to build. Betsy is being tested. But she continues to have her eye on the big prize, knowing that three months...six months...a year of fighting are well worth the effort for a lifetime that lies ahead.

In honor of Betsy's 100th day, Julia brought her a paper chain of one hundred colorful rings linked together to decorate her room. Julia was so excited, running into Betsy's hospital room with her gift in a large paper bag. As I hung the rings over the windows, I thought about what they really represent. This long string of interlocking circles serves as both a visual reminder of each of the days since the transplant, and as a symbolic reminder of how interconnected we are with each other and with all of you during this fight. It's impossible for us to say how much your love and support have meant through this process.

· · · · · · · · · · · · · · · · ·

The 100-day mark is more than just a symbolic moment, it also gives you your first detailed look at the results of the transplant. In Betsy's case it gave us a reason to celebrate.

The bone marrow biopsy showed no signs of any remaining cancer cells, and no abnormalities that could lead to a relapse. According to this analysis, Betsy was cancer-free.

After all that Betsy had been through, and was still dealing with, it was actually hard to get myself to use the words, "cancer-free" as I updated people with this news. I also had to caution them that as great as the results of the biopsy were, we were by no means out of the woods. Statistically, Betsy would not be able to call herself "cured" until five years after her transplant. The 100-day results were exciting, and encouraging, but all they really said is that we were on the right track. Now we had to keep moving ahead toward that ultimate prize.

The excitement of the test results was somewhat mitigated by the continued challenges Betsy was facing at the time. Her GVHD seemed to be improving. Her energy level was getting a little better. She was introducing broth and Jell-O back into her diet without significant issues. Yet she was still in the hospital, still connected to monitors, and still facing an uncertain path to home.

Weeks passed with minimal progress. Doctors couldn't predict when we would be able to go home. We knew our treatment options were shrinking every day, and we crossed our fingers for definitive proof of a light at the end of this long, winding tunnel.

I had used up all of my vacation and personal time during Betsy's first hospital stay, so this time around I had a different routine. I would go to work in the morning, then head straight to the hospital after work to see Betsy and have dinner with her. Most of the time I was the only one eating, but I would spend a couple hours at her bedside.

I would then head home to get the girls down to sleep. This was my rejuvenating time. Molly and Julia could make me smile no matter what was happening at the hospital. Reading to them, snuggling them, and getting them to bed was a ritual that was at least as valuable to me as it was to them.

Once they were asleep, I would head back to the hospital for a few hours. When she was up to it, Betsy and I would sit together and listen to music or watch a movie. Often this was our quality time when she was most awake and alert. There were some nights when she was less alert and she slept. Then I would listen to music, hold her hand, and hope that being there was bringing her some level of comfort and healing. At the very least, it was comforting me.

As Betsy started to show signs of improvement, the doctors started to give her "hall passes" to get out of the hospital for short stretches.

One day I took her out shopping for a few hours, just the two of us. It may not sound like much, but the chance to do something "normal," unrelated to life in the hospital, was extraordinary.

A couple of times I brought Betsy home for surprise visits with the girls. The first time we walked in the door together unannounced they were so excited. They jumped around the room and squeezed her as hard as Betsy could stand in her weakened state. It was wonderful to see the joy on their faces, and to see Betsy's face light up with a huge smile of her own.

A few days later Betsy was able to go home to see Julia and Molly dressed in their holiday outfits. We had been out for a "Santa brunch" that morning, so the girls were decked out in special long coats and hats. Betsy wasn't able to join the brunch, but she thoroughly enjoyed the fashion show from the girls.

It's generally not a good idea to set goals in a cancer fight, when things are extremely unpredictable and out of your control, but as the weeks passed and Betsy appeared to be doing better, I know we both wanted her to be officially home for Christmas.

On December 22, that wish was granted. Betsy was officially discharged from the hospital after a seven-week stay.

As we packed up her room, took the pictures off the wall, and walked out of the BMT unit, there was a strange sense of déjà vu. We bid farewell once again to the incredible nurses who had led us through this latest challenge. This time we vowed to keep our promise to only come back to the unit to visit, not to stay.

Julia and Molly couldn't stop smiling when Betsy came home. Julia declared it to be the "happiest surprise ever!"

Seven weeks is a long time. Adding in Betsy's first stay for the transplant, Betsy spent three full months away from home that first year. Her joy at being home with the girls reflected that time away.

The simple fact is that there is no remedy for separation other than being together again. As strong and brave as the girls were about having Mommy in the hospital, it was easy to see how much it meant to them to have her home. The first night she was back, when I went upstairs to get into bed, I found Julia had brought her blankets into our room, crawled up into the bed and was tucked up tight next to Betsy. Even as they slept, you could feel how content they were, curled up, mother and daughter together.

We didn't have any illusions that our work was done, but we were thankful to be back together.

Having Betsy home for Christmas was a true gift. Christmas Eve dinner, unwrapping presents, writing a note to Santa, and setting out some cookies (and carrots for the reindeer)—all of these rituals felt more complete and meaningful with Betsy there to share in, and add to, the joy.

On the surface, New Year's Eve that year was the most mundane celebration we could remember. We watched a movie with Julia, put the girls to bed, and then sat and talked until Betsy tired and went to sleep. There was no champagne, no Dick Clark, and no fireworks; the only midnight kiss was the one I gave Betsy's forehead as I climbed into bed long after she was asleep.

But our understated greeting of 2006 didn't diminish our joy at bidding farewell to a difficult 2005, and welcoming a year we fully expected to be among our best.

CHAPTER 20

. . . .

A New Routine

Being home was a huge change, and mostly it was for the better. Instead of nightly hospital visits, we got to curl up as a family to read bedtime stories to the girls.

In the middle of the night, rather than being interrupted by nurses needing to check Betsy's vital signs, we were only awoken by Julia, carrying her blanket into our room to crawl into our bed for snuggles.

Betsy's mom and I took on more active caregiver roles. We were soon fairly adept at hooking up drugs and nutrition bags to Betsy's catheter each day.

Betsy was by no means done with doctor visits. She had to go in multiple times each week to have her blood counts monitored. She often received infusions that would take hours to administer.

Soon after New Year's we had our first visit with Dr. Miller since Betsy's second hospitalization. We were eager to see him to get a feel for how Betsy was doing and what we could expect next. What he told us was sobering.

We asked him whether Betsy's hospitalization had changed her long-term outlook at all. Would she still be considered "cured" at five years? Would there be long-term effects from her GVHD?

He paused, looked at us with a serious expression, and said, "Let's not get ahead of ourselves."

He told us he was pleased just to have Betsy out of the hospital. He said most of the time, when patients are in the hospital at day 100 they don't ever make it out of the hospital.

"I want you to focus on one thing right now," he said. "See if you can stay out of the hospital for thirty days. If you can do that, then let's work to stay out of the hospital for another thirty days. That's all I want you to worry about right now."

It was difficult to hear, but it was also exactly what we needed to understand. We refocused on the task at hand, and on the smaller goals in front of us.

We made it thirty days. Then we made it another thirty days, and so on. It was by no means smooth sailing, but we felt good about defying the odds once again, and we counted each month that passed as a new victory.

There's a strange phenomenon that happens sometimes where an experience in your own life can make you suddenly and acutely aware of that same experience going on all around you.

Have you ever decided you want to buy a certain car, and then started to notice the car *everywhere*? Or you finally settle on a name for your baby and suddenly everywhere you look someone else has already used that name?

This phenomenon can be amusing or mildly irritating when you're talking about cars or baby names. Unfortunately, cancer seemed to create the same effect for Betsy and me, and it was awful.

Before Betsy's diagnosis we knew people with cancer. Some close family friends had cancer, and some had died. I obviously knew how terrible cancer is, but when Betsy got cancer, something changed.

All of a sudden it felt like cancer was everywhere. Friends, family members, parents at our daughters' school, and coworkers all seemed to be getting diagnosed.

I couldn't help but wonder: Is there an epidemic of cancer going on? Or is it possible that I simply wasn't aware of how prevalent cancer is? Was I really blissfully ignorant when so many people around me were struggling?

The reality is probably a little of both. At our age, we were naturally more and more likely to have friends and family members get sick. I also know there must have been times when a cancer diagnosis slipped through my consciousness without the attention it deserved.

With this new consciousness, Betsy and I try our best to reach out and offer support whenever we hear of a new diagnosis. We still aren't always as engaged as we should be, but on some level everyone fighting cancer is on the same team. We add their names to our roster. We pull for them and cheer them on, and we hope that at some point the roster will stop growing. We have plenty of teammates already.

. . . .

CaringBridge Update: Wednesday, January 25, 2006

Betsy's progress right now is measured first and foremost by the fact that she is still out of the hospital. At the end of December, Betsy's doctor told us it would be a positive step forward to simply keep her home through January. Now, with about a week to go, Betsy is still home, she is only going in to the clinic every other day, and she is eating well enough that we've been able to discontinue her catheter feeding. Needless to say, these are great signs.

While the momentum is going in the right direction, we are also aware of the significant risks that Betsy still faces. Right now, the biggest challenge is getting Betsy off of the high-dose steroids that she has been on to control the graft-versus-host disease. Steroids are not something you want to be on for long periods of time, but due to the severity of Betsy's GVHD, her doctors have been very careful about reducing her steroid dose too quickly.

Steroids act a lot like a large bandage in that they can cover up issues in your body, such as GVHD, and prevent them from getting out of control. When you start to taper the steroid dose, it's like slowly unwrapping a bandage—you never know when you're going to uncover an issue that will flare up and cause problems.

Betsy's steroid taper hit a bump in the road a few days ago when all of a sudden her hemoglobin count dropped. Her blood counts had been steady for quite some time, so the drop was a surprise, and was probably caused by a drug interaction that had been masked by the steroids. Betsy got two units of blood, and the doctor raised her steroid level back up. It's a little discouraging to have to increase the steroids again, but we need to do what is necessary to keep Betsy on this narrow path of recovery.

Despite the hard work that continues, we have been extremely grateful for the progress Betsy has made and the mere fact that she is home. Last week saw two major events that drove home just how fortunate we are to be together as a family—we celebrated Julia's fourth birthday, and Betsy's sister, Jane, got married.

Julia's celebration included a birthday dinner (complete with a butterfly birthday cake) and a birthday breakfast with the traditional birthday frittata (with four candles in it). At school they had a celebration where all Julia's classmates made wishes for her and blew them into a tiny box that she gets to keep.

It meant so much to have the family together for the celebration. Julia has been a constant source of strength for us. It may seem odd that we get so much strength from someone so young, but every single day she lifts us up. Putting her to bed each night and listening to her questions, thoughts, and songs is like instant therapy and a release from the stress of the day. We are so proud of her and grateful for her.

Jane's wedding has been an event on the horizon, and in many ways a goal for us, since the moment Betsy was diagnosed. Originally the wedding was going to be in Chicago, but Jane moved it to Minneapolis to increase the probability that Betsy could be there. Even though Betsy wasn't feeling as good as we had hoped she would by this time, this wedding was just what the doctor ordered.

Julia and Molly were both flower girls, and they looked so beautiful. Molly was able to walk the entire aisle by herself, and she loved every second of it.

Betsy was going to stand in the wedding but decided to err on the side of caution and instead sat in the front row. It was a beautiful wedding, capped off by a reception in the exact space where Betsy and I were married. Betsy rested for much of the reception in a room away from the crowd, but was able to come down for a couple of dances.

To be able to dance with Betsy in the very room where, six and a half years ago, we took our vows and shared our first dance as husband and wife was a moment I'll never forget.

. . . .

There are long stretches during a cancer fight when progress is difficult to measure. These are the times when "normalcy" starts to creep back into your life, often unnoticed. Still, "normal" moments, no matter how big or small, are worth acknowledging and celebrating when they are particularly hard won.

The initial months after Betsy's homecoming were marked by constant struggles to stay healthy. The side effects of her medications were extremely difficult to bear, but she had no choice but to push forward.

Weeks would pass without any significant signs of change, but when we stopped to think about where we were just a few months before, we could see remarkable progress.

In many ways, we started to see a reemergence of the old Betsy. She started working on small projects around the house. She was finally enjoying food again. And there were times when I would hear Molly and Julia laughing hysterically in another room and I had to smile, knowing that their mommy was getting back to her entertaining self.

Another significant moment of normalcy came on Valentine's Day when, for the first time since her transplant, Betsy and I went out for dinner. We made a 5:00 reservation to avoid crowds, but we were out together for the first time in more than six months.

Sitting next to each other and enjoying the meal felt so familiar and normal. It was also incredible.

We ventured out for another meal a month later for my birthday, going back to a restaurant we last visited right before her transplant.

I thought about all the steps that brought us back there, and I was amazed at how far Betsy had come. Her hair was just starting to grow back, dark and wavy. She had the old sparkle in her eyes. She looked beautiful.

While much of the evidence of Betsy's progress during this phase was subtle, there were still some milestones that jumped out at us for celebration.

Not long after my birthday, I got home from work and was greeted by Betsy, smiling. She asked me if I noticed anything different about her. It was easy to see. She no longer had the tubes from her Hickman catheter hanging down from beneath her collarbone.

Betsy's doctors decided she no longer needed the catheter because she wasn't requiring as many transfusions and tests. So after nearly seven months, the catheter was removed.

This amazing device had served its purpose, saving Betsy from countless needle sticks, but we were really happy to see it go. It was another step toward normalcy, and it felt like the close of a major chapter in our story.

. . . .

CaringBridge Update: Tuesday, April 4, 2006

When we started on this journey we were told to expect a long fight with many ups and downs. That assessment has proven to be extremely accurate. Over the last couple of weeks the road we were on has taken a detour as Betsy has been battling a troublesome virus. So far she is doing okay, but we ask all of you to once again lend your strength to help us get pointed back in the right direction.

The cold that I mentioned in the last update turned out to be RSV, a respiratory virus that is only a problem for infants and people with compromised immune systems. The primary concern for Betsy is that RSV can turn into pneumonia, which would send Betsy back to the hospital for treatment. If she develops any fever or shortness of breath, we are instructed to call the clinic immediately.

In an effort to head the RSV off at the pass, Betsy participated in a clinical trial to test a possible drug to treat the virus. For five days in a row she had to go to the clinic, eat a high-fat meal (to aid with the absorption of the medicine) and then consume a liquid that was either this new medication or a placebo. Betsy was eager to participate in the trial, both to try to get rid of the RSV and to help advance the research.

One immediate thing we learned from the study: consuming an extremely high fat meal is not as easy as it sounds. The meal had to be at least eight hundred calories, with 50 percent of the calories coming from fat. Day one Betsy had to eat an entire Whopper with cheese. Day two: a personal pan pizza and a few handfuls of cashews to get to the required fat level. Day three, I decided to offer moral support by joining her for a Whopper, Jr. with cheese and large fries. It was a sacrifice, but it was the least I could do! Day four was eggs Benedict with extra hollandaise. As you can see, it takes a lot to get *that* high fat, and when you *have* to finish the entire meal, it's not easy!

(Side note: *one* slice of French silk pie would have accomplished the task, but Betsy isn't a French silk pie fan. I am. Or I was. I think I have officially sworn off French silk pie.)

We don't know if Betsy was getting the actual drug, and we don't know if the drug is effective. All we know is that, so far, Betsy has been able to stay out of the hospital.

To complicate matters, both girls have been sick. Molly probably had RSV as well and has been battling a bad cough. She is just now getting better. Yesterday Julia developed a bad cough and fever. We're keeping the girls away from Betsy and doing a lot of hand washing around the house. Hopefully all the bugs will be gone soon.

Despite the virus, Betsy has been making progress with the tapering of her steroid dose. She's down to a more manageable level where we should start to see some of the side effects start to fade. The tapering may be adding to her loss of appetite, nausea, and drowsiness, but it's worth it. Getting off the drugs is an important step in this process.

Another step that may not be as important medically but is a nice step psychologically came a couple days ago. Betsy went in for her first haircut! It wasn't really a full cut, it was more of a trim or a "clean up" to make sure she is trending to a stylish Natalie Portman look and not veering toward what she called "mullet territory." Still, it was another step toward normal life, and she came home looking great.

Betsy's birthday is on Thursday, and we have reservations at a restaurant for another early dinner. We're hoping her energy and appetite will take a positive turn so we can go out, but no matter what, we will celebrate. We have so much to be thankful for.

Betsy's last birthday was shortly before her diagnosis, and since that time she has been faced with challenges we never imagined. Through it all, Betsy has shown a strength of spirit that has been inspiring. Cancer has not diminished her basic kindness, compassion, and love of life, but instead has illuminated these qualities for more to see. I've been proud of the way she has fought this disease, and I look forward to being at her side to share the victories to come.

. . . .

CaringBridge Update: Tuesday, April 25, 2006

Recovery from a bone marrow transplant requires a delicate balance. You want some graft-versus-host disease to help wipe out the cancer, but too much can cause serious issues. Antirejection medications help prevent GVHD, but they have troubling side effects and create a high risk for infection. Too much activity brings concerns about germs and illness. Too much isolation can be difficult to tolerate emotionally and physically.

Over the last few weeks, Betsy has been able to stay on track, but maintaining that delicate balance takes a great deal of strength, patience, and support.

The best news from the last few weeks is that Betsy's RSV is gone. Whether it was due to the experimental drug she took (and the doctor-mandated high-fat meals), or it was simply that the virus ran its course, we were relieved to kick the RSV and avoid any hospital time.

Unfortunately, Betsy is now dealing with another issue. Nausea and a general run-down feeling are keeping her in bed much of the day and making it difficult for her to eat. We don't know what the cause is yet. It may be a virus (there are many going around right now) or there's a chance it could be graft-versus-host disease flaring up. If it's a virus, her doctors will try antibiotics to keep it under control so she can fight it off. A flare-up of GVHD would be scary because it would require Betsy to go back on high-dose steroids, negating the progress she's made with tapering her medications.

Easter Sunday was an example of how progress and setbacks can define a day. Julia and Molly woke up early, and Betsy dressed them in special Easter dresses to hunt eggs. The girls looked beautiful, and I couldn't have been more proud, not only of Julia and Molly, but also of Betsy as she helped lead them around with their Easter baskets.

After the hunt, however, Betsy was exhausted. By the time we got to her sister's for brunch, Betsy didn't feel up to sitting at the table. Instead, she had to lie on the couch and have a plate of food brought over. I know Betsy gets discouraged when she can't fully participate in activities, but at the same time, she realizes it's a long-term goal that we are moving toward. There are many egg hunts and brunches to come.

After nearly a year of fighting, the sheer scope of this battle can be frightening and overwhelming. To be honest, when we started this journey, both Betsy and I thought she'd be feeling better by now than she does. There are days when Betsy is simply sick and tired of being sick and tired, but we try to keep some perspective by remembering how far we've come.

· · · · · · · · · · · · · · · · ·

CaringBridge Update: Sunday, May 21, 2006
It isn't for the moment you are struck that you need courage but for the long uphill climb back to sanity and faith and security.
-Anne Morrow Lindbergh, 1906 - 2001

My sister-in-law, Amy, passed this quote along about a week ago, and I felt that it painted a perfect picture of where we are right now. We are climbing, but the progress is slow, and the physical and emotional challenges can take a toll.

One ailment that has become a concern recently is joint pain in her wrists, elbows, ankles—pretty much throughout her body. The doctors say it could be a side effect from reducing her medication, or it could be graft-versus-host disease. With all the things going on in her body, it can be tough to pinpoint what causes a particular issue. We just have to watch it and hope it starts to improve.

While the day-to-day progress is slow, there are still milestones to cherish. Betsy got a big lift the other day when she and a friend managed to walk all the way around Lake of the Isles for the first time in nearly a year. They took their time and paused every once in a while, but they made it. The excitement in Betsy's voice when she called me with the news made my day. She did it again a couple days later with her sister and a friend, and again today with her mom. These simple steps—walking a path around a lake—have been a huge boost for all of us during a challenging stretch of this journey.

The other big event of the last couple weeks was Mother's Day, a day that allowed us to reflect on all that has changed in the last year.

Mother's Day a year ago is the last event that I can vividly remember before Betsy's diagnosis. I have found myself looking at the pictures from that day—the brunch at the Mill City Museum, the girls playing with their cousins, group shots of the moms and daughters smiling and laughing—and I can't help but think about how we had no idea Betsy was walking around with cancer. We had no idea what we would experience before another Mother's Day would come around.

Despite the many changes we experienced, Mother's Day this year also was a good reminder of what has been constant: Betsy continues to be an unwavering source of love and comfort for her girls. I know it is difficult for her to let go of many aspects of day-to-day parenting while she recovers, but I try to remind her that there is a deeper level of being a mom that she provides every day. Julia and

Molly have made it through a difficult year and they are happy, confident, and caring girls. As proud as I am of them, I am just as proud of Betsy for the way she has never let her illness dampen her expressions of love to her girls.

An extra Mother's Day toast went out this year as well to Betsy's mom, Susan. If ever there was a demonstration of unwavering maternal love, we have seen it over the past year. Susan has put her life on hold and moved to another state, endured her first Minnesota winter in nearly a decade, and has provided love, comfort, and care that have been instrumental in Betsy's recovery. I don't know how we could have done it without her.

· · · · · · · · · · · · · · · · ·

CHAPTER 21

. . . .

One Year

The one-year anniversary of Betsy's diagnosis brought a mix of emotions. In many ways it felt like we had been fighting the battle for a lot longer than a year. It was hard to not be a little discouraged that Betsy wasn't feeling better and further down the road to recovery.

At the same time, the one-year mark was a huge accomplishment. After all, Betsy's initial prognosis was measured in months without treatment. To be able to start marking years off the calendar felt pretty good.

Betsy's doctor was starting to be pleased with her progress. For the longest time, every time Dr. Miller would come into our room at the clinic, he would sit hunched over in his chair, his hand on his forehead, deep in thought. I figured that was simply his bedside manner. But a funny thing happened as Betsy started to stabilize and improve. Dr. Miller started sitting back in his chair. His hand no longer rubbed his forehead. He smiled a lot more. We always liked Dr. Miller, and we were particularly pleased to see his concerns start to wane so his more relaxed persona could emerge.

When Dr. Miller told Betsy it was okay to start taking small steps out in the world, to be around people again, our first stop was Julia's school.

Betsy had missed most of Julia's first year. She wasn't able to do drop off or pick up. She never got to watch Julia bound down the hall to class, or come running out of class at the end of the day.

So when we left the clinic that day, we drove to school and walked through the doors together. When Julia came out of her classroom and saw Betsy was there to greet her, she ran full speed into her momma's arms for an extended and excited hug. I couldn't tell which of them was happier.

Unfortunately, that victory was followed closely by a setback that put us back on our heels.

Betsy's one-year bone marrow biopsy found something. It was a small abnormality, but it appeared to show some cancer cells in her marrow that somehow survived the chemo, radiation, and GVHD.

Dr. Miller's hand was back on his forehead as he talked about possible next steps after the biopsy. We could put Betsy back on Gleevec to try to get her into long-term remission. Unfortunately this wouldn't be the "cure" we were hoping for. There was no way to know how long the Gleevec would work.

A second option was to take Betsy off of her antirejection medications to spur more GVHD and hopefully kill these stray cancer cells. Considering that her last major bout with GVHD nearly killed her, this didn't seem like an appealing way to go.

The third option would be to go back to her donor to harvest "leukocytes," white blood cells which can be used to spur GVHD to try to wipe out the cancer.

We decided to go with option A. So, a year after her first round of Gleevec, Betsy started back on this drug hoping it would once again perform.

Even after the setback, Betsy and I were determined to keep living life and enjoying the fruits of the progress she had made. She planned a surprise vacation for us for our seventh anniversary. We also made our annual trip to Michigan with Betsy's family. Betsy's condition varied greatly week to week, but she made the best of it. Still, it was hard not to get discouraged.

Betsy described this situation best when she said it was like running a marathon, and just as the finish line was appearing on the horizon, they added ten miles to the race. Nevertheless, she was putting one foot in front of the other.

One of the goals Betsy and I set during her treatment was that as soon as we could, we would find ways to give something back to the organizations that helped us along the way.

About a year after her transplant, we had our first opportunity. We decided to get involved with the Light the Night Walk, an annual fundraiser for the Leukemia & Lymphoma Society (LLS).

LLS was instrumental in helping Betsy in a number of ways. First and foremost, they have invested tens of millions of dollars every year for leukemia research. It was research funded in part by LLS that led to the development of Gleevec, and without Gleevec, Betsy's story would have been very different.

LLS also provides a great deal of information and support to families who receive a blood cancer diagnosis. I used their website often in the initial weeks after Betsy was diagnosed to get up-to-date information about CML and bone marrow transplants.

The Light the Night Walk takes place at dusk. Walkers carry illuminated balloons—white balloons for cancer survivors, red balloons for supporters, and gold balloons in honor of those who have been lost to cancer.

When Betsy decided to form a team for the walk, it immediately energized her. She sent letters, recruited friends and family, and set ambitious fundraising goals. I could tell how important it was to her to connect with people whom she had been separated from for so long. The response to her efforts was overwhelming.

Team Betsy quickly grew. Thirty...forty...fifty people signed up, and the number was still increasing. Just as important, people were contributing generously to the cause.

When the night of the walk finally arrived, Team Betsy numbered more than eighty. Betsy stood proudly behind her registration table welcoming each member of her team. In a way, it was like a coming out party for her. She had been in isolation for so long, she hadn't seen many of these people since before her diagnosis.

When it came time to take a team photo before the walk, we had to squeeze together around her Team Betsy sign to fit everyone into the picture. It was a festive atmosphere. I soaked it in.

The walk itself was beautiful. The sea of balloons was beautiful and poignant. Seeing so many people whose lives have been impacted by cancer made us even more determined to keep working for more cures, more treatment, and more hope for everyone facing this fight.

I watched Betsy walking around the lake with a group of her friends, talking and laughing. I watched Julia marching at the front of our team, holding one end of the Team Betsy banner with a huge smile on her face. I saw the long line of friends and family members carrying their balloons in support of Betsy. The entire scene took my breath away. This is what we had been fighting for.

Betsy completed the three-mile walk, which was a victory. She was exhausted, but exhilarated.

As wonderful as the event was, the results of the walk were even more remarkable. When the numbers were tallied, Betsy was the number one individual fundraiser in the state, raising more than $13,000. Team Betsy was the number one team in the state, beating out even the corporate teams and raising more than $36,000!

From the moment of her diagnosis, through the transplant and the long and difficult recovery, I was always proud of Betsy. Watching her walk that night, talking and laughing with her friends, I couldn't help but be struck by how far she had come. Once again, she managed to amaze me.

The final months of 2006 were a microcosm of the roller coaster ride that defines many cancer fights.

Betsy regained some sense of normalcy. We were able to take a vacation to Florida with my family, where we walked the beach together, searched for seashells, and watched dolphins and manatees swimming in the ocean.

When Betsy was in the hospital we used to talk about things we were looking forward to, and a trip to the ocean was near the top of the list. Sitting together, watching Julia and Molly play in the surf, we felt we had reached a significant milestone. But milestones are not finish lines, and despite the progress we had made, Betsy was still struggling with some significant issues.

Betsy's condition during this period would change week to week or even day to day. She was having trouble eating enough and was losing weight. She also started to have issues with her blood counts again, which forced her back to the clinic for transfusions.

Betsy's doctor started to suspect many of Betsy's issues were being caused by the Gleevec. He tested the theory by having her stop taking the drug for ten days. Betsy immediately improved.

Considering the variety of issues Betsy was experiencing on Gleevec, and the uncertainty about whether or not she was really at risk for a relapse, Betsy's doctors decided to take her off of Gleevec altogether. It was a little scary to move forward without this safety net, but the results were hard to ignore.

Immediately Betsy's energy level went up. She was able to eat. The old spark returned to her eyes.

The timing of Betsy's improvement couldn't have been better with Christmas right around the corner. The year before, just being home from the hospital was the fulfillment of a Christmas wish. This year, Betsy was able to fully participate and enjoy the season.

One of my favorite things about Christmas is the sense of awe and wonder that it inspires. I love the look on the faces of Julia and Molly as they come down the stairs Christmas morning to find that Santa ate the cookies, drank the milk, and left the gifts they wanted. It's a simple moment of joy, surprise, and appreciation.

On this Christmas in particular, I shared that same sense of awe and wonder as I watched Betsy come down the stairs with the girls. To think of where she was a year before, six months before, or even two weeks before, and to now see her leading her daughters down the stairs, holding their hands, a bright smile on her face, it felt like a true Christmas miracle.

. . . .

CaringBridge Update: Sunday, January 7, 2007

In any battle with cancer there are numerous milestones. Sometimes they're moments to celebrate, like coming home from the hospital. And sometimes a moment of great progress can actually be bittersweet. That's the kind of milestone we passed this weekend when, after more than nineteen months of living with us, Betsy's mom moved back to Chicago.

The day that Betsy was diagnosed, her mom got on a plane to come and help. None of us had any idea how long she would be here. She moved into our guest room, and Betsy's stepfather, Duane, started a regular pattern spending half his time in Chicago and half with us in Minneapolis.

Throughout the diagnosis, treatment, and recovery, Susan has been an incredible source of emotional support and stability for our home as we have navigated our way through this unknown and unwanted journey.

You can imagine how hard it is to watch your daughter go through everything that Betsy has gone through. But Susan never let herself be consumed by anger, despair, or desperation, even in the really tough times where any of those emotions would have been easy to succumb to.

One of the most visible testaments to Susan's valuable contributions to this fight is in the way that Julia and Molly have thrived during such a difficult time. Susan was an important source of stability for the girls during the months when Betsy was in the hospital. I would come home for a couple hours a day to eat with them or tuck them in at night, but other than that Susan was handling everything. There's no way to adequately say thanks to someone for assuming such an important role in such difficult circumstances.

Whenever anyone asked Susan how she was handling her care-giver role, she always said, "Where else would I be? My daughter needs me." So the fact that she has moved home is obviously a good sign that things are going well, and Betsy is doing better. At the same time, we know that if a need arises, Susan will be more than willing to come back to help. We hope and pray that she won't have to, and that her future visits will be strictly of the pleasurable variety.

It's important to stop and appreciate signs of progress. Whether it's a big sign, like Betsy's mom moving home, or a small one, like today, when Betsy happily declared that she is off enough medications that she can now fit all of her pills into a smaller pill box, rather than the monstrous one she's been using for the last year and a half. (The "small" pillbox is still filled to the top…but progress is relative).

We know it's going to be an adjustment now that Susan is gone, but we're happy to be in the position to try to figure it all out, and we remain thankful for the incredible support system of family and friends that continues to help us move ever closer to "normal."

. . . .

CHAPTER 22

· · · · · · · · · · · · · ·

Vigilance

· · · · · · · · · · · · · · · · ·

CaringBridge Update: Sunday, January 28, 2007

"You're doing great. We'll see you in six weeks."

That's how Betsy's doctor greeted us when we went in for the results from her last bone marrow biopsy. It was Betsy's first biopsy since she was taken off of Gleevec, so this was obviously welcome news. Betsy's mom had come back to town for the appointment and Betsy's sister was there as well. You could almost feel the collective sigh of relief when we heard the news.

When we left the doctor, Betsy and I decided to make a visit to the Bone Marrow Transplant Unit to see some of the doctors and nurses who helped us get to where we are today. I remember talking to one of the nurses about what it's like when former patients come back to visit. She laughed and said, "We don't get a lot of visits from former patients. I think when people leave here, they are so happy, they don't ever want to come back."

I assured her that we would visit and was excited to live up to those words. It was a little strange to pass through those doors again, but it was certainly nice to walk in by choice, not necessity.

We happened to stop in on the day that one of our favorite nurses was celebrating her birthday. It was great to see her and share our good news. I think many of the nurses and aides were surprised to see Betsy, particularly now that she has hair and looks more like herself.

As happy as we are with Betsy's progress, there are some issues that we are trying to get a handle on. The biggest issue right now is Betsy's weight. Even though she's eating better, Betsy is losing weight to the point where it is becoming a significant concern.

We're not exactly sure why her weight is dropping, but it may be due to chronic graft-versus-host disease. Somehow GVHD may be preventing Betsy's body from properly absorbing the nutrition of what she eats. We need to get a handle on the cause quickly so we can start reversing the trend and help Betsy get her strength back.

. . . .

Life after a bone marrow transplant requires a special kind of vigilance. You need to keep an eye out for any sign of trouble. You can't get lulled into security by a few good weeks or even a few good months. Even a small issue could be an indication of something significant that could throw you off course.

That's what happened with Betsy about eighteen months after her transplant.

Being off Gleevec was agreeing with Betsy, and she was making strides. The girls' spring break was upon us, and we were looking forward to a vacation in Arizona with our families. Betsy, Julia, and Molly flew out early to spend some extra time with Betsy's mom and stepdad.

The day after they arrived, Betsy called me to check in. Everything was great, but she said she thought she got a little too much sun. She had a little rash. I was concerned, but agreed it was probably just from the sun.

The following day, the rash was worse and we started to worry. Betsy called the Mayo Clinic in Scottsdale to try to get into their BMT clinic to be seen. She was told they didn't have any available appointments for six weeks. She explained that she was visiting from Minnesota, was a BMT patient, and she had no way of knowing she would need to be seen six weeks ago. Couldn't they fit her in? They told her if she was having a problem she should go to the Emergency Room.

As good as the Mayo ER probably is, they aren't BMT doctors, and BMT patients are unique. The doctor she saw there didn't understand why a rash would be so concerning. He gave her some lotion to try and sent her home. When the rash continued to progress, Betsy tried the Mayo BMT clinic again, but was again turned away.

We started to get desperate, so we called our doctors at the University of Minnesota, friends who might have connections, anyone we thought could help us get into the clinic.

When I finally arrived in Arizona and saw Betsy, I was frightened. Her rash was all over her body, and she looked very uncomfortable. I was angry that she hadn't been seen by the clinic.

Luckily, we had tracked down a family friend who knew the head of the Mayo BMT program. One call later, Betsy had an appointment the next day.

As irritated as I was about the inequities of our health care system (you should not need connections to see the right doctor), I was relieved that someone familiar with transplants was finally going to see her.

When we walked into the clinic the next day, they took one look at Betsy and immediately decided she needed to be admitted to the hospital.

I knew they were right, and I appreciated that they were taking things seriously, but I was also irritated that it took this long to get some attention. If they had seen her the first day, maybe she wouldn't have gotten to the point of hospitalization.

Nevertheless, there we were, being led once again into a BMT hospital unit.

The Mayo facility was very nice. The room was large. They had large flat-screen televisions and movies on demand. But there were other things that made us uncomfortable after our experience at the University of Minnesota.

First, we noticed that all of the doors to the patient rooms were left open. I asked why that was. In Minnesota, all the doors were kept shut for fear of infection. They said the entire unit was sterile, so there was no need to close the door. That didn't make me feel any better.

The second major difference at Mayo was their policy about children. I brought the girls to see Betsy that night, and I was told children are not allowed in the BMT unit at any time.

"Even if they're healthy?" I asked.

"No matter what," they said. "Too much risk for infection."

At the University of Minnesota they used to have a "no children" policy, but they changed it. They realized that the healing benefits of being able to see your children outweighed the risk of infection, as long as the children are healthy. I agree with this position, having seen firsthand how a visit from Molly and Julia used to lift Betsy's spirits, even during difficult times.

Mayo didn't agree, but I'll bet some of their patients would have gladly traded the open-door policy for a chance to see their children.

As a compromise, we were allowed to bring Betsy out of the unit to a waiting area to see the girls. It wasn't ideal, but at least Julia and Molly got to give Betsy a hug and see that she was okay.

Once we were settled in, attention turned to figuring out what was wrong with Betsy. It didn't take long for the doctors to determine Betsy was having a significant flare-up of graft-versus-host disease. The most concerning discovery was that, in addition to causing a skin rash, the GVHD was attacking Betsy's liver as well.

Betsy ended up spending three somewhat surreal and uncertain nights in the hospital, getting high-dose steroids and other GVHD treatment. We were grateful to be at a good facility, but after more than fifteen months out of the hospital, it was discouraging for Betsy to be back in that environment, hooked to an IV and anxiously waiting for signs that her treatment was working.

There were times during this hospital stay that were as scary as any we had experienced. Knowing the GVHD was attacking a major organ made us pretty scared. The doctors were consulting with Betsy's doctors at home, but being in the unfamiliar environment with doctors we didn't know added to our anxiety.

Luckily Betsy's rash and her liver numbers started to improve after about forty-eight hours of treatment. She was discharged on her birth-day. Reuniting with Julia and Molly and celebrating with a dinner out with our families was the best present either of us could imagine.

When we returned home and checked in with Dr. Miller, he joked with us about having such an eventful vacation, and we came up with a plan where we would notify him of any travel in the future so we could have a list of doctors and phone numbers we could call just in case.

· · · · · · · · · · · · · · · · ·

CaringBridge Update: Tuesday, May 22, 2007

Ever since Betsy's diagnosis, we have talked about "normalcy," a time when we can put CML behind us and get our old lives back. But what we have learned is that "normal" is relative. It's not really about get-ting our old lives back. It's about moving forward with a new appre-ciation for moments that are only possible because of all the fighting that has come before.

Over the last few weeks alone we have attended Julia's first bal-let performance, spent a pre-Mother's Day night at a beautiful bed and breakfast, attended T-ball games and Twins games, and watched Molly joyfully embrace swimming and gymnastics lessons. Two years ago, moments like these seemed like a distant dream. Today, they are a new version of "normal." For now this version includes things like prednisone, blood tests, and biopsies, but we're thankful for where we are, and we are optimistic about the future.

· · · · · · · · · · · · · · · · ·

The highs and lows of a cancer journey are something you start to get used to after a while. It's really no different than regular life, other than the highs can sometimes feel higher and the lows can definitely knock you back on your heels.

A couple months after our Arizona adventure, we experienced both ends of the spectrum. Betsy had a once-in-a-lifetime experience, and we got some devastating news about one of the heroes we had met in the BMT.

Through my job at Best Buy, I got tickets to the Police concert when they came to Minnesota on their reunion tour. Being children of the '80s, Betsy and I were huge Police fans.

Since I had worked on the public relations plan around the tour, I also scored VIP passes to go to the sound check before the show.

There were about seventy-five people watching the sound check, and, to our surprise, the band started asking people to come up on stage to sing with them. I thought about raising my hand to volunteer, but singing in public isn't my strength. I was shocked when I saw Betsy's hand shoot up in the air to volunteer. The next thing I knew, she was up on stage right next to Sting, singing lead vocals to "Roxanne."

Despite having a cold that made her voice a little raspy, she belted the song out with gusto. Sting gave her a hug and a kiss on the cheek. Later, at the meet and greet with the band, Sting said to Betsy, "I remember you—you're a good singer!"

I had two thoughts. First, I wished that I had overcome my fear and had joined Betsy on stage. Second, it showed how Betsy's fight with cancer had changed her perspective. Betsy's not a singer or performer by nature, but she jumped at the chance to get up on stage with the Police. When she saw the look of surprise on my face she simply said, "When am I ever going to get this chance again?" She had a good point.

Betsy told me that before her diagnosis she probably would have thought too much about getting up on stage, and she would have talked herself out of doing it.

There aren't many positives you can point to about a fight with cancer, but a willingness to embrace life's opportunities without hesitation is perhaps one of the few nice side effects.

To this day, whenever the song "Roxanne" comes on the radio, our whole family sings along with gusto, remembering Betsy's moment in the spotlight with Sting.

This was part of a positive stretch for Betsy. She was feeling good. We were able to get out and about for fun events. (We even saw Prince in concert *twice*, but sadly he didn't follow Sting's lead and call her onstage to sing.) We made it back to Michigan with Betsy's family for vacation.

But the positivity of this stretch was tempered by some news we received upon our return from Michigan.

Our friend Bonnie, who had received a transplant at the same time as Betsy, relapsed.

We were shocked and saddened by the news. Bonnie was an inspiration to us throughout Betsy's transplant and recovery. Her prognosis after the relapse was grim, but we prayed for a miracle for her and her family as they geared up for another big fight.

CHAPTER 23

. . . .

Giving Back

Throughout Betsy's transplant and recovery, we looked for ways to give back, to help raise awareness of issues related to leukemia, or to encourage people to get involved. The Be The Match registration drive we held was one example that ended up paying dividends beyond what we could have imagined.

Joining the registry is easy. Today you can do it by simply swabbing your cheek and sending the sample in to Be The Match.

The importance of the commitment you are making when you sign up is much more serious. As we saw with Betsy, time is of the essence when one needs a transplant. Individuals who sign up for the registry but later decide not to go through with it when they are called, potentially put someone's life at risk.

Our bone marrow drive registered 143 people as potential donors. We were thrilled with the response, and we crossed our fingers that perhaps one of those donors would someday get a chance to save a life.

To our surprise and delight, so far *three* people from that drive have been called upon to donate.

The first was a childhood friend of Betsy's. About a year and a half after Betsy's transplant, Andy got the call, and he enthusiastically accepted. He went in for tests to verify the match, and he donated stem cells to a young woman.

It was interesting to see the process from the other side, and it was heartening to see how the experience profoundly impacted Andy.

Unfortunately, the woman who received the cells didn't make it. Still, Andy's donation accomplished more than even he can imagine.

He gave that woman hope. He gave her family hope. He allowed her extra time to fight and to spend with her loved ones. I don't know anything specific about her story, but as a spouse of a recipient, I can tell you that Andy's gift was priceless, no matter the outcome. Luckily, Andy understands this. He has remained very active with the Be The Match Foundation, telling his story and encouraging others to sign up.

About a year after Andy was called, a childhood friend of mine was told he matched a patient. Deacon also accepted the call with enthusiasm. He donated stem cells, and while we don't yet know the outcome, he would tell you the act of donation was one of the more meaningful things he has done.

To our amazement, a third person from our drive was also called to donate more than five years after the drive. Betsy's mom received this e-mail from a friend of hers letting her know:

"Christina got the news yesterday that she was chosen to donate stem cells for a thirty-eight-year-old woman in Spain. It never ceases to amaze me that a young man in Germany can help a young mother in Minnesota, and now a woman in Minnesota can help a woman in Spain.

She is very excited to donate. She and I signed up to be donors at the drive arranged when Betsy needed a donor. It was the day before Christina's wedding. I'll never forget it."

We've seen so many amazing things come out of Betsy's experience, but knowing that we managed to touch the lives of three patients going through similar stories with this one donor drive is among the best feelings we can imagine. The Be The Match donor drive is a tangible example of how we were able to pay it forward and take something positive from Betsy's illness.

Another positive that has come from our experience has been our involvement with the Leukemia & Lymphoma Society's Team in Training (TNT).

TNT is a program that trains participants to compete in endurance athletic events such as marathons, triathlons, and century rides. The athletes pledge to raise a certain amount of money, and in turn, they get to participate in team practices and receive coaching and the benefit of staff members to take care of all the travel and logistics for the event.

I am not by any stretch an "endurance athlete," but through TNT I have participated in six events:

- two sprint triathlons
- a century ride around Lake Tahoe with my brother
- a marathon
- a half-marathon in San Francisco.

None of these challenges were easy for me, but they were incredibly rewarding, as I told my supporters after the first of these events:

July 17, 2007
Dear Friends and Family,

About six months ago, I made a decision that was met with more than a little surprise. Ignoring my natural aversion to running, biking, and particularly to swimming, I signed up to do the Lifetime Fitness Triathlon. Some of Betsy's friends did the triathlon last year as part of Team in Training to raise money for the Leukemia & Lymphoma Society. Watching them last year inspired me to give it a try. I figured if the chance to raise money and help fight blood cancers couldn't get me off the couch, what would?

So around January, I started attending swim drills with Team in Training. I bought the first pair of "running shoes" of my life. And I got my bike tuned up and ready to go. I had July 14 circled on the calendar as the day I would swim four-tenths of a mile, bike fifteen miles, and run three miles—all in one day—one after the other. It was my attempt to give something back to an organization that has done so much in promoting research that has literally saved Betsy's life.

Team in Training provided great coaches and mentors aimed at helping even the most inexperienced triathlete (me) prepare for and finish the race. Despite the fact that I could hardly swim one lap without resting, and couldn't run a mile without stopping and walking, they assured me I would be able to complete my goal.

Throughout the months of training I learned some important lessons: It really is a bad idea to eat a big meal before swimming (it took about half of a length of the pool for this lesson to be learned. Yikes). When you're running after swimming, it's important to use a product called "Body Glide." (Double yikes.)

And perhaps most important, when you're buying your first pair of "triathlon shorts" it's good to look closely at the tag. I found this out after buying a pair that I liked and working out in them, only to have Betsy say, "Are you sure those are men's shorts?" I reacted indignantly and assured her they were, only to learn upon closer inspection that Danskin does, in fact, specialize in "premium athletic apparel for women." I guess the female triathlete on the tag should have been a clue. In my defense, the shorts were awfully comfortable.

As the weeks went on, I made strides forward, like the first time I ran around the lake without stopping (an approaching thunderstorm helped me along), and setbacks, like the time when we were on vacation in Michigan and I kicked a rock during a swim, requiring stitches on the top of my foot for a nasty puncture wound.

All along, I was supported by Betsy, who encouraged me to keep training, and Julia and Molly, who would cheer for me as I headed off to swimming lessons. Julia used to say, "Good luck, Daddy! I know you're going to win the triathlon!" Thankfully, she came to understand my definition of winning was to finish, and she was just as enthusiastic about this goal as well.

The culmination of this work came on Saturday when I donned my official Team in Training triathlon suit for the event. Just going out in public in this suit was an act of some resolve. Suffice it to say, it doesn't leave much to the imagination. When I first tried it on, Betsy laughed for ten minutes straight. I couldn't blame her.

I got to the site of the triathlon at 4:30 Saturday morning to set up my "transition area," where I would switch from the swim to the bike ride, and later to the run. We then gathered as a team for encouragement and to remind ourselves why we were doing this event. Betsy was one of the "Team Honorees" for the triathlon. Many of the athletes followed her story and dedicated their training and fundraising to her. As we went around the circle, 132 people talking about their reasons for doing Team in Training, I was touched and very grateful to be part of this group.

The race started, and I waited anxiously for my heat to take off, the 35- to 39-year-old "short course" racers. At about 9:30, I got into a single-file line that was dispatched one at a time into the lake.

The swim started off as planned. I ran into the water and used a couple of "dolphin dives" to get into the deeper water just as I had been taught. That was the last part of the triathlon that went exactly as planned. I started crawling through the water past the first couple of buoys and looked up to see where I was, and realized that the course was a lot longer than it looked from the shore.

My goal on the swim, as with the entire race, was simply to go at my own pace and finish. I wasn't trying to keep up with every-one else. It was immediately apparent that trying to "keep up" wasn't even going to be an option.

Each wave of racers is given a different color swim cap, allegedly to help keep track of the swimmers. From my perspective, all it did was make it obvious just how many swimmers were passing me by. I started out in a group of dark blue caps. After swimming a short distance, I looked around and saw nothing but red caps surrounding me, as my fellow dark blue swimmers disappeared into the distance. The next time I looked up, a sea of yellow caps was passing me by, followed a hoard of green caps. The parade of colors continued until finally I looked around and was back with a group of dark blue caps—not from my group but rather the one five heats behind me. At least

I was able to pretend I was keeping up for a few minutes before this second wave of blue also passed me by.

After about twenty-five minutes, I made it back to the beach, stumbled ashore to the loud cheers of my family, and ran to get onto the bike where I had my second lesson in humility.

For some reason, all triathletes get their race number written in marker on their arms, and their age written on the back of their calves. I have no idea why they write the ages down. On the bike ride, all this did was alert me to the relative age of people speeding by on their bikes. Whether they were younger or older was no consolation. I would watch a fourteen-year-old ride past and lament lost youth. Then I would see a fifty-nine-year-old go by and wonder why *my* relative youth wasn't serving me so well. Still, I made it through the bike route and transitioned to the final run.

It was near the beginning of the run that I had a moment that reminded me what I was doing there. I had written a message to Betsy on the front of my triathlon jersey. As I ran by, a woman yelled out, "You can do it! Betsy is counting on you! You're her hero, and you're my hero too!" I almost had to stop running. The fact is, Betsy is *my* hero, and at that moment it felt so good to be doing something for her, in her honor. It was the exact boost I needed to get to the finish.

The bottom line is that I did finish. My time was slow, but I made it—and with the help of many of you I raised more than $8,500 to fight a terrible disease. I got to be part of an amazing team—many of them with their own personal reasons for fighting leukemia, others with no personal connection who simply wanted to do something to help others.

When I signed on for the triathlon, I was sure it would be a one-time challenge. Now I'm not so sure. Being able to do something to show my support and admiration for Betsy's fight meant even more than I imagined it would.

I may try again next year. But no matter what, I am grateful for the team, for all the people who donated money to support my effort, and for the incredible example of strength and perseverance that Betsy sets for me every day. As usual, I couldn't have done it without her.

Brian

Team in Training continues to be an important way for Betsy and me to take an active role in supporting leukemia research. Every time we sign up for an event it is an amazing adventure, and we hope our efforts will help researchers get closer to the most important finish line: a cure for all blood cancers.

CHAPTER 24

. . . .

Celebration and Loss

. . . .

CaringBridge Update: Wednesday, August 15, 2007

On August 24 we will mark the two-year anniversary of Betsy's bone marrow transplant.

The two-year mark is a major milestone, and Betsy's checkup earlier today provided definite cause to celebrate. Her most recent biopsy once again showed 100 percent donor cells in her marrow and no sign of a relapse. Her doctor said we couldn't ask for a better two-year report. We couldn't have been more appreciative of the news.

Over the last weeks, Betsy has started to feel more and more like herself. Her graft-versus-host disease has been under control, and some of the symptoms have started to improve. She has been able to reduce her prednisone dose to a maintenance level instead of the high levels that were causing so many side effects. If the GVHD stays under control, she may be able to start tapering off of the immuno-suppressant drugs altogether by next spring.

A true testament to Betsy's improvement came during a recent trip the two of us took to California. We met up with my college friends in Carmel for a few days, and then the two of us drove up to Napa for two nights. We finished up back with college friends in San Francisco. It was a very busy vacation, and Betsy never missed a beat. We went out for nice dinners, did some wine tasting, and even saw Barry Bonds hit home run 758 at AT&T Park. Betsy was able to enjoy it all.

It seemed fitting to take such an amazing vacation right before her two-year anniversary. As we drove through the wine country together, I couldn't help but think how nice it was to be with her, having new experiences and fully enjoying the life that she has worked so hard to live.

The importance of savoring each moment was driven home in another way at the end of our trip. Sadly, we found out that our friend Bonnie lost her battle with leukemia last week after efforts to bring her back into remission failed.

Coincidentally, Bonnie lived in San Francisco, and her memorial service was on the day we were flying home. We attended the service, where her husband gave a heartfelt and moving tribute to Bonnie. As emotionally difficult as it was, we were grateful to be able to be there to honor a woman who touched our lives deeply and to lend our support and love to her wonderful family. We will always keep them in our thoughts and prayers.

. . . .

Bonnie's death was one of a few that hit us particularly hard during Betsy's fight. Three good friends battled hard and lost, and in the process, they illustrated some basic truths about courage, cancer, and how a disease can both create and curtail a legacy in one fell swoop.

Bonnie

The first time Betsy met Bonnie face to face was in the BMT unit in the middle of the night. Betsy had a troubling fever and had to be whisked off to x-ray to see what was going on in her lungs. This was during a time when Betsy was in quarantine and hadn't seen anyone but family, nurses, and doctors in weeks.

The door to Betsy's room opened and she was wheeled into the hall just as the patient next door was being wheeled back to her room. It was Bonnie.

Bonnie and Betsy knew *of* each other. Bonnie was from San Francisco and was our age. She and her husband, Mike, had two daughters similar in age to ours. We had numerous friends in common from various connections, so when Bonnie was referred to the University of Minnesota for treatment, we were told to look out for Bonnie and Mike.

We hadn't been able to meet before Bonnie went in for her transplant. When Betsy went in, we inquired about Bonnie, and it turned out she was in the room next door. Betsy wrote a note to Bonnie and asked a nurse to deliver it. They exchanged a few notes back and forth when they felt up to it, but they still hadn't met.

It wasn't exactly a storybook first meeting. Betsy was coughing uncontrollably in her wheelchair. She looked up and saw Bonnie in another wheelchair. They looked like twins with their freshly bald heads and facemasks covering everything but their eyes. Bonnie lifted her hand in a tired wave to Betsy. Betsy did her best to return the gesture, and that was it.

We didn't see Bonnie again for a few more weeks, but I did see her husband and daughters in the halls when they came for visits. I remember thinking how hard it must be for all of them to be separated by such distance during this ordeal. My heart went out to them for the added stress and separation they had to endure.

When Betsy and Bonnie both got out of the hospital, we started to see more of her, mainly at clinic checkups. They became friends immediately.

Bonnie had an infectious smile that made her eyes sparkle with energy even when she wasn't feeling particularly energetic. She had been battling leukemia longer than Betsy, trying chemo first before relapsing and needing a transplant. Despite the long road, she was a force of positivity. She made people laugh, and she never seemed to let the day-to-day grind of her long recovery get the best of her.

After a few months, Bonnie got to return to San Francisco, so we would only see her when she had her required checkups back in Minnesota.

To be honest, there were times during that first year when seeing Bonnie and her husband was a little discouraging. We couldn't help but compare Betsy's progress with how Bonnie was doing, and Betsy was obviously not doing as well.

Bonnie got off of her medication when Betsy was still on heavy doses.

When we met them for dinner one night, Bonnie walked in looking so healthy and radiant, you would not have known she was sick. Betsy was still struggling with significant GVHD.

We, of course, were thrilled for Bonnie and Mike. We tried not to get discouraged, remembering every case moves at its own pace. We also looked at Bonnie as an inspiration, glad to see that it's possible to go through as much as Bonnie had and come out looking so wonderful. She was a hero to us.

The news of Bonnie's relapse hit us square in the gut. It was apparent almost immediately that she wasn't going to be able to beat cancer this time around. It was just going to be a matter of time.

Time meant months in Bonnie's case. And knowing this, Bonnie approached the end of her life with the passion, energy, and positivity that defined her.

She made plans. She planned for her daughter's future. She planned for Mike's future. She helped everyone else along her path. She remained a hero.

We felt lucky to be able to attend her memorial, but it was difficult. When Betsy and I pulled into the parking lot at the church, the first thing we saw was Bonnie and Mike's daughters walking in the front door. They were wearing beautiful dresses. Their hair was made up. They reminded me so much of Julia and Molly that I had to catch my breath.

Betsy and I stayed in the car for a few minutes to gather ourselves. Then, finally, we took a deep breath, walked in to see Mike, and said goodbye to Bonnie.

Todd

One of my earliest memories of Todd is from an engagement party that my old boss threw for Betsy and me when I was working at a PR agency.

Todd had recently started as an intern, and while I knew him, we hadn't spent much time together.

I remember him telling me he was bringing his girlfriend to the party. When he said this he looked at me with one of those "I'm going to marry her" looks that young men often get before they are old enough to realize their first love is rarely their final love. Later, at the party, I saw Todd and Karen together for the first time, and I realized this wasn't youthful naïveté. Todd and Karen appeared to be the exception to the "first love rule."

The other thing I remember about that night was being genuinely struck by Todd's maturity, thoughtfulness, and wisdom beyond his years. Part of the evening involved everyone in the room giving "advice" to the engaged couple. As various people spoke, and it was getting to be Todd's turn, I remember wondering what he was going to say. What kind of marriage advice could a guy right out of college impart?

I wish I could remember exactly what Todd said, but all I remember is that he blew me away. He stood up and spoke confidently and eloquently. He spoke from the heart, which isn't always easy in your early twenties, and I knew right then and there that Todd was a very special person.

Todd got cancer a couple of years after he and Karen got married. He noticed some pain and a bump on his arm. It was osteosarcoma, a terrible bone cancer most often found in kids.

When Todd first got sick, I didn't really know what to think. This was the first time cancer had touched me in this way, with a good friend who was so young and healthy at the time.

Todd had surgery. They replaced his forearm with cadaver bone to try to get rid of the cancer. This was about a year before Betsy was diagnosed, and this time my naïveté was in full effect. I thought the surgery did the trick, and Todd was out of the woods. It was difficult to watch him go through it, but I really figured that was the end of the story.

When Betsy was diagnosed, Todd's shining example was an inspiration to me. Cancer could be defeated. Betsy and I were going to follow his lead.

Then, a few months after Betsy's transplant, I got a terrible call. Todd's cancer was back. It was in his lungs.

Todd and I were supposed to participate in a fantasy basketball draft that night. Todd loved that league. I told him I would draft a team for him so he could still be in the league. He declined.

"If I stay home tonight I'm just going to think about cancer, and I'm going to be sad to miss the draft," he said. "I've got plenty of time to think about cancer, but if I miss having a team, I'm going to regret it all season long."

He came out that night, and we had a chance to talk. By this time, I had a better understanding of what he was going through. We shared a bond and a common enemy.

But we didn't just talk about cancer. We also had a chance to just enjoy being together. We drafted our teams. We laughed. It meant a lot to have him there.

Betsy and Todd ended up fighting cancer side by side. During Betsy's second hospital stay, Todd was two floors up, getting chemo.

Stopping in to see him on my way to or from the hospital was surreal, to say the least. Sometimes Karen and I would talk, both of us with the faraway gaze of a caregiver in our eyes. I remember appreciating the chance to be with someone who understood what was going on, and to exchange words of support and encouragement to someone who was as in need of those sentiments as I was.

During one of Betsy's really difficult stretches, I told Karen that every time I left Betsy's room I would kiss her on the forehead and whisper "keep fighting" in her ear. Karen understood, and it helped me beyond words to know that.

The paths that Todd and Karen, and Betsy and I took seemed to ebb and flow as cancer gave us each unique challenges. We took turns being the "strong couple," the example showing that cancer can be overcome.

There were stretches when I wouldn't see Todd for a while. Then, when I would see him again, I was always surprised by how good he looked. He could always muster a million dollar smile.

Todd had a remarkable ability to keep smiling beyond a time when most of us would be able to. At our last basketball draft together, Todd was in so much pain he could hardly sit. Still, he made it through the night, and he got a twinkle in his eye on the way home when he was listing his players and asking my thoughts on some of his "sleepers." After all he had been through, he still had a smile in his eyes and an infectious enthusiasm.

The writing was on the wall for quite a while, but Todd's death still surprised me. He had pulled off so many amazing recoveries I expected he would always persevere.

Todd's determination to not allow cancer to rob him of experiences defined his battle. It was a devastating fight that went on for six years.

When people are very sick for a long time, you often feel relieved when they pass away and are at peace. I didn't feel that way about Todd. When someone loves life that much, it doesn't seem right to take it away. I miss him terribly.

Emily

Emily was a friend of mine in high school. She was a couple of years younger than I. She was easy to get to know, and easy to like.

I lost track of her for a long time after high school, but I had heard she moved to Napa Valley. She married a man whose family owned a vineyard.

Betsy and I stopped at their vineyard during our trip to San Francisco. It was the same trip when we found out Bonnie had died. By chance, Emily was visiting family in Minnesota while we were there, but we did reconnect via e-mail. A few months later, that's how I got the news: Emily was diagnosed with lung cancer.

Once again, I was shocked and saddened by the news. Emily had never smoked in her life. She exercised regularly. By all accounts she led a very healthy lifestyle. How could this happen?

Despite my experience with Betsy, I still ask these kinds of questions. Part of me still wants to believe that cancer can be controlled or predicted. The random, almost willfully unpredictable, nature of the disease is one of its most frightening characteristics.

I sent Emily some notes of support and started following her on CaringBridge. Her sister wrote most of the updates, and I was amazed by the energy and humor that they brought to Emily's fight.

Emily was in an advanced stage of lung cancer when she was diagnosed, so the prognosis was grim. Still, from the very beginning, she and her family left no doubt they were going beat it.

There were many times when it seemed like she was winning. She had a ton of support from her husband, her two young daughters, and devoted family and friends. But every time it looked like things were getting better, a new scan would show new spots, and new treatments were needed.

Slowly those treatments took their toll. Nerve damage impacted Emily's ability to walk. She went from limping, to a walker, and finally to a wheelchair. Still, the cancer kept growing.

In the midst of it all, Emily started working to raise money for cancer research. She was the honoree for the V Foundation Wine Celebration in Napa Valley, an event that raised more than $700,000. A foundation in her name continues to fund critical research, hoping someday we can beat lung cancer for good.

Emily fought for four years before she died. She dealt with a great deal of pain and emotional stress, but she continued to laugh, smile, and make those around her feel special.

The stories of these three friends illustrate a few basic truths about cancer.

The fact is, when it comes to cancer, strength, courage, and positivity guarantee nothing.

People who say they "willed themselves" to a cure, or that they simply *refused* to let cancer win, are failing to recognize a simple fact: There are people who are just as strong, just as positive, and who love life just as much as they do, who die.

This doesn't mean attitude isn't important. To the contrary, I believe that how you approach the battle is incredibly important, both in terms of helping your body fight and what you gain from the journey along the way. However, I think we do a disservice to those who are struggling in suggesting that things might be different if they were more positive or if they "wanted it more."

The second truth that Bonnie, Todd, and Emily reinforced is that as powerful as cancer is, the human spirit is stronger.

All three of my friends rose above their illness to inspire others and to make a difference. They used the time they had left to leave a lasting impact on the world. They did this by raising money and awareness to fight their diseases. They did this by reaching out to family and friends, letting them into their lives, and inspiring us to make the most of whatever time we have. Finally, for Bonnie and Emily, they did this through their children. They poured their hearts and souls into their kids until the very end. It's not easy to be a mom and to be sick, but they made it a priority to leave their children knowing their moms love them very much.

Finally, the stories of my friends debunk another grand myth: that somehow cancer can give more than it takes by inspiring people to do great things and leave a legacy.

It's true that Bonnie, Todd, and Emily will be remembered. Memorials in their names and events in their memory continue to raise extremely important funds for cancer research. The lessons we all learned from them and their inspiring courage will live forever with those who knew them.

Still, the fact is that they were each taken from us far too soon. Who knows what incredible things they could have accomplished with another forty or fifty years of life?

Saying cancer is a gift gives the disease too much credit, and too much power. Bonnie, Todd, and Emily were gifts. Cancer couldn't change that, but it did deny us more time, more experiences, and more potential from these amazing people.

CHAPTER 25

. . . .

Positive Momentum

. . . .

CaringBridge Update: Tuesday, October 2, 2007

There are many ways to measure progress in a cancer fight. There are the medical milestones. There is the passage of time without incident, knowing every day that passes takes us closer to being "cured." Then there are the moments, often small, that provide certain proof that all the effort, all the fighting, is paying off.

For Betsy, one of those moments came a few weeks ago, on Molly's first day of school.

As we got the girls ready, Julia eager to see her friends, and Molly nervous and excited about this new adventure, I thought back to Julia's first day of school two years earlier.

On Julia's first day, Betsy was in the hospital for her transplant. I tried to capture the moment for Betsy, taking photos of Julia on the front step, lunchbox in hand, a smile on her face. I brought Julia to school and watched her march down the hall, not bothering to look back over her shoulder at me, simply jumping into this new experience. I went straight to the hospital to show Betsy the pictures and to tell her how it went. We were so proud, but I know it was painful for Betsy to miss it.

Even after Betsy got out of the hospital she wasn't able to be a part of Julia's school experience. Because of her weak immune system, Betsy couldn't go into the school. She couldn't interact with the other parents. She couldn't participate in school functions.

Betsy used to ride in the car with her mom to pick Julia up at the end of the day, but she had to stay in the car while her mom went inside to wait for Julia. Betsy told me how hard it was to sit in the car with the windows up, watching all the other parents walking into the school and coming back out holding the hands of their children, listening to their stories about their day.

As she sat there, waiting, she made a promise to herself that she was going to get there. She would do whatever it took to share that simple joy with her daughters.

So as Julia started her third year of school, and Molly got set for her first year, Betsy was determined to soak up every moment.

This time around, Betsy helped get the girls dressed in their special "first day of school" outfits. She fixed their hair. The girls posed for pictures that were meant for posterity, not for immediate sharing with someone who couldn't be there.

We took Molly off on her new adventure together, as a family, and we watched our little girl march off down the hall toward class for the very first time.

For Betsy, this was more than a milestone. It was a well-deserved and much-needed reward for two years of hard work.

. . . .

CaringBridge Update: Monday, November 26, 2007

The most important news is that Betsy is feeling good.

The most dramatic evidence of her progress came during her last doctor appointment about a month ago. We went in for a routine checkup, and she got a great report. Then, when we asked about the scheduling of her next biopsy, we got an answer that took us both by surprise.

"Things are looking good. You're now two years out from your transplant. So I don't think we need to do any more biopsies unless we see something in your blood that makes us want to take a closer look."

When we heard this news, I think both Betsy and I nearly fell over with surprise. Betsy has been having bone marrow biopsies every three months since her diagnosis. They're no fun. So now, to be able to put this procedure on the shelf and not have that "next biopsy" hanging over our heads was an unexpected and very welcome relief.

Aside from bidding farewell to biopsies, the other exciting news for Betsy is that she has finally connected with her stem cell donor. Because her donor was from Germany, international regulations required Betsy to wait two years before trying to contact him. Shortly after that two-year date passed, she learned that his name is Tobias. He agreed to allow Betsy to get his contact information, so she was able to send him an e-mail. They have written back and forth a couple of times now. He doesn't speak English, but Betsy has friends who have helped her with translations.

It's hard to explain the emotion of hearing from Betsy's donor, and how important it has been for her to be able to express her thanks. This is a man who saved Betsy's life. He was nineteen years old when he gave this gift to a complete stranger. So to learn something about who he is and to be able to let him know what a difference he has made in the lives of so many people has been an incredible experience.

. . . .

CaringBridge Update: Saturday, March 29, 2008
Just to give you an idea of how much better Betsy has been feeling, over the last month we have:

- Attended a huge costume party dressed as Juno and Bleaker (from the movie *Juno*). The picture will be posted on the CaringBridge site. Warning: I'm wearing VERY short running shorts. The picture is not for the squeamish.
- Celebrated my fortieth birthday (yikes) with a surprise trip to Chicago. Betsy set it up without my knowledge and took care of every detail—concert tickets, art institute tickets, and reservations at great restaurants.
- Celebrated my fortieth birthday AGAIN (hey, you only turn forty once) with a party at my parents' place. Betsy actually took classes at the Apple store to surprise me with a "this is your life" slideshow set to music for the party. She worked

very hard on it and it turned out great. It was a very special night.

- Had dinner with Kelly, one of our favorite BMT nurses, and her boyfriend—an amazing chance to spend time together not as patient–caregiver, but as friends.

When you throw all these things together you start to get a picture of "normalcy," or at least something pretty close to it.

. . . .

July 17, 2008 (Team in Training – Part 2!)

If you had asked me a couple of years ago, the only thing that would have seemed more preposterous than the idea of me completing a triathlon would have been the idea of me completing *two* triathlons. But last weekend I once again put on my tri suit, slathered on the Body Glide, and participated in the Lifetime Fitness Triathlon on behalf of Team in Training and the Leukemia & Lymphoma Society.

Year two of my triathlon career proved to be just as adventurous as year one. I had my training interrupted by a nasty bout of pneumonia (and learned just how hard it is to swim while coughing uncontrollably). I injured my ankles running on worn out running shoes. (I had never owned running shoes before. Who knew they had to be replaced so often?) And I had the humbling experience of accidentally joining the "fast lane" during swimming lessons one night. It wasn't until my lane mates started passing me like I was treading water that I realized the farthest lane is set aside for advanced swimmers only. Oops.

Having one triathlon under my belt did help me train better this year. I learned a lesson from my slow-motion bike ride a year ago and invested in "clipless" pedals and bike shoes for a more efficient ride. While the new pedals helped, they did take some getting used to. While practicing clipping my shoes in and out of the pedals (simply standing still in my back yard), I lost my balance and took a fall into a group of hostas. Thankfully, no one saw this graceful training moment.

Another aspect of the triathlon that I had to reacquaint myself with was—yes—that skintight outfit. While I was able to avoid any incidents of tri suit cross-dressing this year, I did have to get used to wearing those shorts again. When I returned from my first bike ride and run wearing my new outfit, I asked Julia what she thought of the shorts. She said, "I guess they're good for when you go running, Daddy...but if you wore them to someplace like the airport, I don't think that would be appropriate." Looking in the mirror, I had no choice but to agree.

Despite the minor setbacks and ego-bruising moments during my training, working with Team in Training was once again an amazing experience. Before each swim lesson we would pause for a "mission moment," where team members would offer thoughts or stories to remind us why we were working so hard. I heard inspirational stories of triumph over leukemia, and heartbreaking tales of people participating in memory of loved ones who lost their fight. I was proud to be a part of the team.

Two nights before the triathlon, Team in Training holds a pasta dinner to get everyone together to celebrate. There were two speakers at the dinner. One was a thirteen-year-old boy who is the team honoree this year. He just finished his treatment and is in full remission. He looked great and spoke optimistically about his story despite having to endure such exhausting and debilitating treatment. He was a shining example of how far leukemia treatment has progressed.

The second speaker was a woman who bravely recounted the story of her husband's unsuccessful battle with leukemia. He fought hard and survived long enough to witness the birth of their second child. Team in Training is her outlet to try to bring something positive from her experience. She gave a compelling speech and reminded us all of the work that still needs to be done finding cures.

The night before the triathlon I took a black marker and wrote tribute messages on my triathlon jersey to remind me of the real meaning behind this undertaking. I wrote Betsy's name on the front, and then names of friends who are fighting cancer or who have lost their battles on the back. I was struck by the number of names I had to write. As I wrote them down, I paused to think of each of their stories, their courage, and how they have inspired me to do whatever I can to help more and more people beat these diseases.

Race day started early once again this year, with a 3:00 a.m. wake-up call. My race time was an hour earlier than last year, most likely because I was now part of the forty-four-year-old age bracket and they probably feel we need a little more daylight to complete the race. I finally hit the water at about 9:00.

You would think my experience would have prepared me to handle the start with ease, but in the rush of adrenaline I actually forgot to put my goggles on until *after* my first dive into the lake. Then, once I got the goggles on, they fogged up, leaving me with limited, blurry vision for my swim. About fifty yards into the race, I had that old panicked feeling again thinking there was *no* way I was going to make it. Not the best start, but I was able to calm myself down and slowly start making my way across the lake.

Saturday was a beautiful day for a triathlon—not too hot or humid. It was windy though, and that meant choppy water. A couple of times (after treading water for a little rest) I got hit with a wave and a huge mouthful of water just as I was taking a breath to start moving again. This was usually followed by the next wave of swimmers kicking, splashing, and bumping me as they cruised by. I had to stop, gather myself, and try again.

The bike ride (with my new pedals and shoes) went fairly smoothly. I was a little worried about getting on and off the bike without a repeat of my backyard incident, but I was thankfully able to execute with minimal drama.

The length of the ride was once again a challenge. My training rides are usually about seven miles, so more than doubling it to fifteen for the triathlon definitely pushes my limits. As I started to wear down, I found myself concentrating on all the names on my jersey, reciting them in my head over and over again and thinking about their long, difficult battles. At one point, half way through the ride, I went over a bridge and could see the University of Minnesota

Hospital up river, the scene of the transplant that saved Betsy's life. I slowly pedaled the bridge, staring at those all too familiar buildings, giving thanks for Betsy's progress and sending best wishes to all the patients currently fighting in that BMT unit. It was just the inspiration I needed to push through the rest of my ride.

The run was a little painful, but I was able to make it without stopping or walking. When I saw my family lined up along the finish line (with Julia and Molly cheering and holding up a sign they had made) it gave me an added boost. I kicked it into second gear (or at least what *felt* like second gear) down the home stretch—ALMOST to the finish line. For some reason I just couldn't keep it up for that last ten feet, and I eased up to cross the finish line. I think my body was simply saying "enough."

At the end of the day, I felt very good about my second triathlon. My times were a little better than a year ago (slightly faster on the swim and bike, a little slower on the run). Most important, it gave me a chance to give something back to the Leukemia & Lymphoma Society to help with research that will lead to more cures.

Thanks to many of you, I ended up raising more than $7,500 to fight blood cancers. I was the top fundraiser on the team this year, and that made me feel better than if I had won the triathlon.

It was an honor to be a part of the team. It was humbling to get so much support. And I was so grateful to be able to celebrate at the finish with Betsy, who has fought a much more difficult challenge for more than three years and is my absolute inspiration every single day.

Thank you all for your support. I can't tell you how much you have meant to Betsy and me throughout this journey.

Brian

———————————

CHAPTER 26

. . . .

Tobias

As Betsy began to feel more and more healthy, she started to dedicate more energy to the Be The Match Foundation. She agreed to co-host the foundation's first gala benefit.

Betsy spent countless hours working on the event, helping plan the dinner, securing auction items, and figuring out the flow of the show.

The evening was a tribute to Rod Carew, the Minnesota Twins Hall of Famer who lost his daughter to leukemia in 1996. One of his daughter's dying wishes was for Rod to continue working to get more donors on the registry. Rod promised her he would, and he has been true to his word. He has been extremely active in raising awareness of bone marrow donation across the country, and works tirelessly getting new donors to sign up for the registry.

Through her role as co-chair, Betsy was able to meet Rod, and she went out on the field with him before a Twins game to raise awareness of Be The Match. Rod then took her around and introduced her to some of the Twins. He's an extremely classy guy.

As exciting as that was, it was followed by news that went beyond our wildest dreams. As part of the event, Be The Match contacted Betsy's donor in Germany and he agreed to fly to Minnesota to meet her!

Betsy was overcome by this news. We always hoped to someday meet her donor. We never imagined it would happen so soon. We were told he was in the middle of his mandatory military service in Germany, and he was able to get a temporary release to make the trip.

The evening after Betsy found out about his visit, we told Julia and Molly about what this man had done—donating his stem cells to help

Betsy fight her cancer. Julia looked at Betsy and said, "So this man pretty much saved your entire life?"

She nailed it.

We couldn't wait to look him in the eye and thank him for the incredible gift he gave to our family.

· · · · · · · · · · · · · · · · ·

CaringBridge Update: Monday, September 22, 2008

What do you say to someone who saved your life? How do you say "thank you" for all of the ways that this person has made a difference, and for all the lives that he has touched through this gift?

It's a question that Betsy has been pondering ever since her bone marrow transplant. And it's the question that we had the distinct honor of addressing last week when Betsy got to meet the young man from Germany who donated stem cells to a complete stranger, and gave Betsy a second chance at life.

As part of a fundraising event for the Be The Match Foundation, Tobias Hoffman and his fiancée, Marleen, flew to Minneapolis from their hometown near Frankfurt, Germany. They arrived last Wednesday, and the five days we had together rank as some of the most exciting and meaningful days we can remember.

The first meeting happened at our house Wednesday night. I flew home early from a work trip to be there, and when I got to our house, the sense of anticipation was electric.

There was a banner in the front yard that Julia and Molly had decorated declaring, "Willkommen, Tobias und Marleen!" There were balloons. Betsy was standing on the front walk talking with a reporter from KARE-11, our local NBC station. Julia and Molly were kneeling on the sidewalk decorating more signs to hang. And Betsy's mom, stepfather, father, sister, and stepsister were all milling around the house, preparing for Tobias's arrival.

About an hour later, Tobias and Marleen arrived. When he got out of the car, I was struck once again by his youth. Tobias is now twenty-two years old. He was nineteen when he donated. I am still amazed at the maturity that would convince someone so young to get on the bone marrow registry and to follow through on that important commitment.

Betsy greeted Tobias with a hug that was three years in the making. The smiles on both of their faces spoke volumes, even as the language difference made for a meeting with few spoken words. Betsy's voice shook a little when she introduced Tobias to Julia and Molly. It was the only moment of the evening when the weight of the last three years encroached on the joy of the moment at hand.

We spent the first evening getting to know each other. Tobias and Marleen showed us pictures of their eighteen-month-old daughter and pointed out on a map where they live in Germany. We walked them around our neighborhood on a perfect late-summer evening. When we asked Tobias if he was surprised to see the television news here when he arrived, he said with a smile, "I didn't realize this was such a big deal."

That night, when I was tucking Julia into bed, she said, "I just think it's so special that Tobias is the one who saved Mommy's life."

Thursday night was the fundraiser. Betsy co-chaired the event with our good friend, Jim Schifman, and they did an excellent job helping organize a special evening.

The evening started with a silent auction, followed by a brief program where Jim and Betsy shared their stories. Betsy looked beautiful, and she absolutely commanded the stage. I thought back to three years ago, or even one year ago, and marveled at how far she has come. Many people who supported us through Betsy's treatment (including the incredible physician's assistant who was one of Betsy's primary caregivers) were in the audience. It felt like a team celebration of Betsy's triumph.

Later in the evening, after a moving video about Rod's story and Betsy's story, Betsy and Tobias took the stage together to a standing ovation from the more than five hundred people in the crowd. It was then that I learned exactly what Betsy would say to the person who saved her life.

"Tobias, danke das du mir das leben gerettet hast. Du bist meine

Held." In English, "Thank you for saving my life. You are my hero." I don't think there was a dry eye in the audience or on the stage. It is a moment I will never forget.

After the first two event-filled days, we got to spend some quieter, quality time with Tobias and Marleen, and while we already knew they had big hearts, we discovered they are a lot of fun as well. They had never been to America before, so we tried to give them a good feel for the Twin Cities. Betsy took them to the zoo where they probably spent as much time laughing and chasing Julia and Molly as they did looking at the animals.

We took them out to dinner, to the Mill City Farmers Market, and for a ride on the light rail out to Mall of America. At the mall, Tobias and I took Molly and Julia on the log ride (judging from a photo of us on the ride, I won the prize for being the most scared). We ate chili dogs, shopped for Levi's, and touched stingrays at the aquarium.

There were moments when it was hard to believe that we were actually hanging out with this man whom we had wanted to meet and thank for so long. But as Tobias and Marleen became more comfortable speaking English and we learned more and more about each other, it became less surreal, and we were able to build a very special friendship in a short amount of time. Tobias and Marleen even invited us to their wedding next fall—a touching offer that we hope to be able to take them up on.

Yesterday we brought Tobias and Marleen to the airport to send them on their way home. Their visit surpassed any expectation we could have had. I watched Betsy give Tobias one last hug, and I felt lucky to be able to witness such a genuine, heartfelt moment.

We've seen so many milestones throughout Betsy's battle with leukemia. The start of chemo, the day she was cleared for her transplant, the day her counts came in, getting home from the hospital…the list goes on. But this time, it was nice to have a milestone that didn't have medical implications or require test results. This was a milestone that was simply about sharing our life with someone to say "thank you."

· · · · · · · · · · · · · · · · ·

There were moments throughout Betsy's journey that seemed like they were more than accidental occurrences. Call them coincidences or serendipitous moments—we were often struck by the way things happened to come together in meaningful ways.

Whether it was Julia's butterfly emerging on the day we confirmed Betsy's donor, or that we happened to be in San Francisco on the day of our friend Bonnie's memorial service, there were moments that seemed too symbolic or too meaningful to be pure chance.

But of all the moments of serendipity, nothing prepared us for the moment in the spring of 2009 when we received an invitation in the mail.

We knew Tobias and Marleen were going to invite us to their wedding in Germany, but we thought it was going to be in the fall. When we opened the invitation, we saw that it was, in fact, going to be in the summer—on June 19—the date of Betsy's and my tenth wedding anniversary.

The coincidence took my breath away. We couldn't imagine a more meaningful or appropriate way to celebrate our first decade as husband and wife.

CHAPTER 27

· · · · · · · · · · · · · ·

Tahoe

The summer of 2009 was eventful, to say the least. In addition to planning our trip to Tobias's wedding, I trained for my third Team in Training event, a one-hundred-mile bike ride around Lake Tahoe. This time I recruited my brother to join me on the adventure. It was much harder than I imagined it would be, but the week before Betsy and I flew to Europe, Mark and I completed our century ride.

· · · · · · · · · · · · · · · ·

CaringBridge Update: Friday, June 12, 2009

Lake Tahoe Recap:

After more than four months of training, hundreds of miles of practice, and an unbelievable amount of support from friends and family, Team Lucas officially completed the Lake Tahoe Century Ride on Sunday.

This was without a doubt the most difficult endurance challenge I have taken on. But when I crossed the finish line, the hard work, anxiety, and even the aches and pains faded (at least temporarily). I simply felt relieved and grateful to have been part of the event. And it was even more meaningful to complete this task with my brother, Mark, riding by my side (even though he made the whole thing look a little too easy for my liking).

When I signed up for the Tahoe ride, I admit I underestimated the task. The longest bike ride I had ever done was fifteen miles (twice—during my triathlons). Still, I was strangely confident when

I started showing up for spin classes in February. When the weather started to warm up in March, and I got outside for some rides, reality started to creep in.

I kept on training and edging my mileage up...fifteen miles...twenty miles. With each new distance I learned about a new biking issue. At thirty miles I decided I needed biking gloves (you really can get numb hands from holding on to handlebars). A thirty-five-mile ride convinced me in no uncertain terms that my old bike shorts didn't have enough padding. Then came the most difficult test: the Iron Man—a sixty-five-mile ride that nearly got me to hang up the biking shoes for good.

The ride took place in 39-degree weather, with icy rain and a strong wind that somehow seemed to be blowing into me for virtually the entire ride. After thirty miles I felt like I was pedaling in quicksand. I was soaked through my clothes. My toes and fingers were numb. And I had thirty-five miles to go.

Mark and I did finish the ride, and some good actually came out of it. First, the ride convinced me to get a new bike. It was obvious my "hybrid bike" was built for comfort, not distance. I needed something that would give me at least a fighting chance.

Second, I learned that if you can just keep the bike upright and the pedals moving, you eventually get to your goal. During the grueling inclines, all I could think about was Betsy, and how she persevered through so many long days with no choice but to push forward. I thought about all the challenges she has overcome, and it kept my feet pushing toward the finish.

When I got my new bike, I could feel the difference immediately, and I started to regain at least a little confidence. I remember once coming back from a fifty-two-mile ride and telling Julia how happy I was that I did fifty miles without feeling too much pain. She responded, "That's great, Dad. But isn't Lake Tahoe going to be twice that long?" Ouch. Who knew math lessons could be so disheartening?

The trip to Tahoe was a whirlwind. Mark and I flew to Sacramento after work, arriving around midnight. We got our rental car and drove to Lake Tahoe, making one wrong turn, and one stop for a late night

In-N-Out burger. The drive was much longer and windier than I anticipated (for a while, I was worried the In-N-Out burger might live up to its
name), but we finally pulled into our hotel at 3:00 a.m. (5:00 our time).

We were up at 6:30 the next morning for a little warm-up ride
with our team. The weather was terrible. It was cold, rainy, and windy.
I started to have "Iron Man" flashbacks. Mark and I went out in search
of some weatherproofing gear, and discovered we weren't the only
ones who were concerned. Hundreds of bikers were crowded into
the shops snatching up gloves, hats, masks, and rain gear.

I decided I could get by with some glove liners and something
to keep my legs warm. I selected a pair of black "knee warmers," tri-
ple-checked that they were NOT made by Danskin (after my first triathlon experience I learned you can't be too careful), and decided
that should be enough to get me through.

Saturday night was the Team in Training pasta dinner, where we
were greeted by hundreds of TNT coaches and staff from across the
country cheering for us as we walked in. It was an incredible moment
that reminded us of the real reason we were there. More than 1,700 riders all came together for a common goal: to find a cure for blood cancers.

Sunday morning we were up at 5:00 to get ready for our 6:15
start time. When we left our hotel room, we were surprised to find
the outside of our door had been decorated with cards, drawings,
and notes of support that Julia, Molly, and Betsy, Mark's daughters,
C.C. and Martha, and his wife, Amy, had sent with our team coordinators. It was the perfect way to start the morning and to ease some of
the jitters of anticipation I was feeling.

Our team gathered together and waited for our start time to
be called. I looked around, amazed at the number of bikers. Many
teams at the ride attach symbols of their home states on their bike
helmets for the ride. The Los Angeles team had Hollywood signs on
their heads. Team Boston attached bowls labeled "Chowdah." Our
team had cans of Spam attached to our helmets, which prompted a
constant stream of questions from other riders. ("Yes, we make Spam
in Minnesota. No, we don't really eat it. Yes, I AM aware they eat a lot
of Spam in Hawaii.")

Finally, the moment of truth arrived and we started on our way. We were lucky. The weather was dry and cool—perfect for the ride. I pedaled down the road not fully knowing what I was in for, but happy to be a part of it all.

The first seven miles were pretty flat. Then we hit the first climb: steep switchbacks. I had been warned to expect this, so I was ready to grind it out. I put my head down and climbed to the top. Mark and I celebrated the successful conquering of challenge number one!

We kept a decent pace going around the lake and felt pretty strong past thirty…forty…fifty miles. I had been told that drinking a lot of water was key when you're exercising in high altitudes. I think it helped, but it also added a whole new level of urgency as we tried to make it from rest stop to rest stop (with sometimes an emergency "rest stop" in between).

We reached mile seventy feeling good, all things considered, and we stopped to eat lunch looking out at a spectacular beach and a stunning Lake Tahoe view. I honestly could have stayed there all day, and knowing the hardest climb was soon to come, it was a tempting thought. Still, I got up from lunch and pushed on for the final stretch. It was as difficult as advertised.

From about mile seventy-eight to mile eighty-six we were climbing—pretty much constantly. I had to once again focus on Betsy, and her strength, to keep me focused and pressing forward. I kept pedaling. I kept climbing. And slowly but surely I made it to the highest point of the ride. Mark and I took a short break at the rest stop and then pointed our bikes downhill toward the finish line.

There were still a few inclines before the ride was over, but they were nothing compared to what we had been through. Soon we saw our hotel, and Mark and I rode across the finish line side by side, huge smiles of relief across our faces.

We finished the ride in just over nine hours. More important, Team Lucas raised more than $13,000 for the Leukemia & Lymphoma Society. The event raised more than $6.8 million.

Mark and I flew out early Monday morning, feeling a little sore, but really good about accomplishing our goal. I was back at work on

Tuesday, putting in a few days at the office before Betsy and I head to Europe to attend Betsy's bone marrow donor's wedding. It will be an amazing culmination of two very meaningful weeks.

Thank you all once again for your support, both for my ride, and for Betsy's journey. We are lucky to have you all in our lives.

Brian

. . . .

CHAPTER 28

· · · · · · · · · · · · · ·

A Trip of a Lifetime

Journal Entry – June 26, 2009

A couple weeks ago, Betsy and I went on a vacation that was more than four years in the making. We left Julia and Molly with Betsy's mom and flew to Europe for nine incredible days, ending in a small salt-mining town in Germany. There, on June 19, we celebrated two special occasions—our tenth anniversary, and the wedding of the man who made that milestone possible, Betsy's bone marrow donor, Tobias, to his bride, Marleen.

Since Betsy's diagnosis with leukemia, there have been countless occasions when I have wondered to myself, "How did we end up here?" We have seen difficult and scary moments where time seemed to stand still. We have shared inspirational moments of hope and celebration. But nothing we have been through quite prepared me for the moment when I watched Tobias and Betsy dance together on his wedding night. Sitting there, I thought back on the long, strange path that brought us to this time and place. It was hard to believe we were really there, but I felt lucky to be a part of it.

Our European vacation started out with four nights in Paris. And, yes, it was just as amazing as it sounds. Betsy and I spent most of our time walking, (or I guess in Paris, "strolling") arm in arm or hand in hand all around the city. We climbed the Arc de Triomphe. We watched the Eiffel Tower light up at night. We enjoyed Bellinis at the Ritz with an old college friend.

In Notre Dame we stopped and lit candles for friends and family members who are fighting cancer. It was sobering to be reminded of just how many people we know who have been impacted by cancer.

Betsy said I didn't have to light one for her, since we had used up so many candles already, but I wanted to light one more to give thanks for the chance to be there together. As I lit the candle and placed it in the stand, I think we were both a little surprised at the emotion that snuck up on us. Four years later, there are still moments when this journey takes our breath away.

Of all the moments in Paris, perhaps our favorite had nothing to do with the city's history or culture. It was during our second afternoon as we walked to a park about ten blocks from the Arc. It wasn't a tourist spot. It was simply a park where families come to play, picnic, and relax. We strolled through the park watching kids kicking soccer balls around and imagined what life would be like living in Paris. The sun was shining. The sky was bright blue. We sat together on a park bench. I will never forget it.

On our fifth day, we left Paris and took a train to Baden-Baden, a beautiful German town near the Black Forest. In twenty-four hours we experienced as much of the town as we could. We took the funicular to the top of the mountain and enjoyed a beer and bratwurst looking out over the landscape. We obeyed the "When in Rome…" tourist philosophy and tried out the famous Baden-Baden Roman baths. I'll spare you the details other than to say it pushed my comfort zone to the limit, and left Betsy laughing at my attempts to make it through with at least a little dignity intact.

That night we played a little blackjack and roulette in a casino that seemed to have stepped right out of a James Bond movie. Think crystal chandeliers, grand pianos, jacket and tie required—I almost asked for my beer "shaken, not stirred" but thankfully resisted the urge.

We left Baden-Baden feeling energized by the adventure and full of anticipation for what still lay ahead.

The following day we took the train to Frankfurt, where Tobias met us at the station dressed in the Rod Carew Twins jersey we gave him when he visited Minnesota. He greeted Betsy with a big hug.

Over the next few days we were treated like family. We were amazed by how quickly we felt like part of the group, and how easy it was to connect with everyone.

The wedding day started with an intimate ceremony. There were only about sixty people invited, mostly family and a few close friends. It was a beautiful ceremony, and it was an honor to be a part of it.

One of the interesting parts of being at a German wedding was to see some of the unique traditions. For example, when Tobias and Marleen left the ceremony, their friends stood in front of them with a large sheet painted with a heart and their names on it. They had to cut the large heart out of the sheet using tiny scissors in order to proceed. It took a while, but finally they stepped through the heart only to find another challenge—a stand with a large log on top and a saw that they had to use to cut through the log. Watching the bride and groom working so hard to saw the log was very amusing, but the symbolism of the two of them showing they can work together as husband and wife hit home with Betsy and me, particularly given the challenges of the last four years.

Once the log was successfully cut, we went to the wedding reception site, arriving around noon. Betsy and I were surprised to find we were seated at the table with the bride and groom and their parents.

As soon as we walked in, we noticed that on one side of the hall there were six or seven long tables filled with about thirty different homemade cakes from family and friends. We figured it was a preview of the after-dinner dessert buffet. Then everyone started grabbing plates and digging in. I had about four pieces of cake to *start* the reception—and the party was on!

The "cake course" was followed a few hours later by a huge dinner buffet. Then came a dessert buffet with mango mousse, pots de crème, and chocolate-covered fruits. A midnight buffet featured entrées, desserts, and of course, more cake.

Aside from the food, the other remarkable thing about the reception was how much of a celebration it was. Everyone danced. There was a lot of laughing. Marleen's dad always made sure I had a fresh beer, and got me to do an ouzo shot with him, (thankfully my only shot of the night). There were fun activities and traditions sprinkled throughout the evening.

Betsy and I had a ball. We got to relive our own wedding reception by dancing to some swing music that someone requested for us. (Sadly, my skills have deteriorated considerably over the last decade.) The local paper interviewed Betsy about coming to the wedding (it was a front-page article the next day). And we finally left the reception at 2:00 a.m., on the shuttle...with all the grandparents. The rest of the guests kept dancing until the music stopped at five. A great party.

The day after the wedding, we got a fascinating tour of the salt mines, traveling through miles of tunnels more than 1,500 feet below ground. Then we went back to the reception site for leftovers from the night before. We said goodbye to our new friends. To see Tobias's grandparents hug Betsy goodbye with tears filling their eyes was moving, to say the least.

On Sunday, Tobias and Marleen drove us to Frankfurt for our flight. It was nice to have some time in the car to talk and reflect on the last few days. At the airport, tears flowed once again as we bid "Auf Wiedersehen" and thanked Tobias and Marleen for an unforgettable visit.

I still sometimes have a hard time believing the coincidence (or fate) that brought us to Germany to celebrate Tobias's wedding and our tenth anniversary on the same night. Betsy and I felt like the trip was a second honeymoon. There could not have been a better way to reflect on an amazing ten years and to usher in our next decade together.

———————————

CHAPTER 29

· · · · · · · · · · · · · ·

Cured

Five years after Betsy's transplant, on her "fifth 'second birthday'," Betsy and I followed through on a promise we made to each other when we were in the hospital. We threw a huge party.

The five-year mark is when the chance for relapse becomes so low that Betsy could finally call herself "cured." That's a word we had waited a long time to finally use.

We had become pretty good about celebrating milestones over the years, and this was the biggest milestone of all. So we rented a space, booked a friend's band (he had generously made an offer to play for this party when Betsy was first diagnosed), and invited everyone.

We went through our address books. We assembled e-mail addresses from CaringBridge postings. We gathered cards and letters people sent, and we did our best to make sure each and every person who touched our lives on the journey was invited to celebrate.

The event ended up being much larger than our wedding, and in many ways it was just as momentous and emotional. Every time we looked up, we saw someone who had had a role on our team coming through the door. There were people who had sent us cards or e-mails to express support. There were friends who had brought us meals, or who did errands to help us through difficult times. And there were others whom we hadn't seen in years, who greeted us with teary hugs and told us how they had been thinking of us and praying for us every day.

Everyone present had played a role. We were humbled and honored to have them there.

Three moments in particular stand out about the night.

The first was when Betsy and I looked over and saw our dear friend, Todd, and his amazing wife, Karen, coming through the door.

By the time of Betsy's party, Todd was in rough shape. Multiple surgeries and chemo treatments had left him reliant on a portable oxygen tank he carried around with him. It was difficult for him to stand.

But when we saw him the night of our party, he was walking with Karen at his side, a huge smile on his thinned and exhausted face. We gave Todd and Karen huge hugs and wiped the tears from our eyes. Todd said he had been feeling pretty awful all day, but there was no way he was going to miss this celebration. He and Karen were able to stay through our slideshow and our speeches of thanks to the guests before Karen wheeled him back to their car to head home.

Todd died six months later.

A second treasured memory from that night is reading aloud a testimonial letter Betsy's doctor sent. He was hoping to attend the party but couldn't be there. Instead he sent this heartfelt and poignant note for me to read to the assembled crowd:

Dear Betsy,

I asked Brian to read this note on this wonderful occasion. I am sorry that I cannot be with you guys to celebrate tonight, but judging by the Evite attendance list, you are not alone.

As the audience does not know me, I will start with a brief introduction, and I promise not to go on forever. (You know I am full of words!) My name is Dr. Jeffrey Miller from the University of Minnesota Bone Marrow Transplant Program.

You, Brian, and I first met for several hours on June 2, 2005. I laughed a little after reading my initial note, because even then, the way you presented was "unique." It's a descriptor that would really define you over the many years we have known each other.

If your CML was routine, we would have just treated you with a leukemia pill called "Gleevec," which allows some CML patients to never think about transplant. You were different…and I can now say this with a smile.

Given all the complexities with your disease, we all agreed that a transplant was your best chance to grow old with your wonderful children, family, and friends.

As those with you today can attest to, this journey was not easy. I am not one to worry, as I am an eternal optimist, but you had me worried on many occasions. All the BMT staff, nurses, coordinators, and everyone you touched took me aside and threatened me to make you better. I kept saying, "Be patient." Little did I know how much patience we would all need.

You reminded me that good things are not always as easy as we would like them to be. You had about as much graft-versus-host disease as anyone can handle. I remember going over your course a thousand times. Did we pick the right donor? Did we choose the right timing? Were we treating your graft-versus-host disease enough, but not too much? These questions are without definitive answers, and they define the art of BMT.

While I was doing all this pondering and worrying and questioning, you managed to stay strong. You always had a great smile, and you never let the situation get the best of you. You are an eternal optimist. This is a sign of tremendous strength, and that is why you are here today.

The only other time you worried me was when you took family vacations. No offense to your wonderful family who is with you today, but after that trip to Arizona when you got sick, I worried about you taking vacations and thought maybe it would be best for you to stay home.

Okay, enough reminiscing. My last heartfelt comment about you is really a thank you. Your birthday represents why I do my job. What you give back is why I do this, why I want better answers, and why I want to see more people like you have "second birthdays." Your smile is the bonus. I wish I could bottle your attitude. I would market it as "Betsy's Cheer," and the world would be a better place.

Thank you, Betsy, for being you, for smiling, and for being strong for me, for your family, and your friends. We all needed you to be strong to help us get through this with you, and you did it!

Happy Birthday, Betsy, and many, many, more. I will have a toast to you at my family gathering tonight.

Be well, and grow old. (Well, you do not have to hurry on the latter part).

Dr. Jeff Miller and the BMT team, who really like you!

The final treasured moment from that night came soon after I read the letter to the crowd. I got off the stage and watched Betsy step up to the microphone to express her thanks to friends and family.

Julia and Molly were on each side of her, giving her a hug. Betsy was the picture of health. She looked beautiful.

After so many weeks and months spent searching Betsy's face for a sign of her "spark" and looking for evidence that the old Betsy was still in there, seeing her that night was like watching fireworks on display. I sat back and enjoyed the show.

Many times, an event that you have been looking forward to for a long time feels anticlimactic after all of the anticipation ends. This was not one of those nights.

Every aspect of the evening was as meaningful and wonderful as we had hoped it would be. Team Betsy was together for one celebratory night. It was an honor to be a part of it.

CHapTer 30

. . . .

It's Not About the Cancer

There are few words that have the impact of the word "cancer." Even spoken in general conversation, the word can make your heart race or your stomach hurt. But when used in relation to a loved one, "cancer" immediately becomes much more than a word, a concept, or even a disease. In that single, terrible moment, cancer becomes a part of your life.

For those who survive cancer, the word often takes on another meaning. Many people come to think of cancer as a gift that gave them new perspective, incredible experiences, and a heightened appreciation for life. I've even heard people say they wouldn't trade their cancer experience for anything in the world.

My wife is a cancer survivor. We had an incredible journey that has changed us in wonderful and unexpected ways.

I would trade it all away in a second.

From my perspective, it's not about the cancer. I believe that much of what you bring out of a cancer fight depends on what you brought into it. Cancer can heighten appreciation. Cancer can bring you new experiences. But for me, cancer doesn't deserve credit for any good that comes in its wake.

When I look at the "gifts" we received from this fight, I can honestly say there are easier ways to gain the perspective, experiences, and meaning that we drew from Betsy's illness. Here are just a few suggestions:

1. Travel. Nothing puts your world, your experiences, and your problems in perspective quite like getting outside

of your world and experiencing someplace else. It doesn't have to be an international trip. You don't have to visit tourist areas. Sometimes simply sitting in a park with someone you love changes your outlook on things.

2. Make connections. I feel lucky to have had the chance to attend Tobias and Marleen's wedding. We had a meaningful, authentic German experience. We witnessed their rituals, we participated in the traditions, and we were embraced not as guests, but as family.

   Our connection with Tobias and Marleen was borne out of extraordinary circumstances, but there are other ways to form lasting and meaningful relationships with people around the world.

   Host an exchange student. Join the Peace Corps. Live in another country for a few months and immerse yourself in the lifestyle. If connecting with another culture is important to you, you can find a way.

3. Seize opportunities. We hear the advice all the time.
   "Seize the day."
   "Live like there is no tomorrow."
   "Make hay while the sun shines!"
   But how often do we actually live by those words?
   It was a "seize the day" mentality that got Betsy to raise her hand to get on stage and sing with Sting. Betsy isn't a singer or a performer, but she couldn't let that opportunity pass her by.
   I'm not going to say that Betsy's cancer has rid me of fear, or that I now leap into every opportunity that comes before me, but her illness has taught me to pause from time to time to gather my own strength and take chances that I wouldn't have taken before.

Do I really live like there's no tomorrow? No. But I at least try to appreciate today.

4. Find a cause and make a difference. Some of the most rewarding elements of our journey have come as a result of our desire to give back to organizations that helped us along the way.

I joined the board of the Leukemia & Lymphoma Society. Betsy and I have raised nearly $100,000 to support cancer research through the Light the Night Walk and Team in Training.

Betsy has worked on the steering committee for the Be The Match Foundation, helping organize their annual fundraiser. It was this experience that opened the door to meeting Tobias.

Working for these organizations has been extremely rewarding, but the most important thing to remember is this: Betsy didn't have to have cancer for us to get involved. Many of the people on my Team in Training teams have had no actual experience with cancer. They would tell you being a part of the team still touched and changed them in amazing ways.

Whether you want to cure cancer or you want to save the tigers in Asia, organizations need your help. Following your passion and making a difference will bring you experiences and rewards beyond anything you can imagine.

5. Accept help when you need it. In any crisis, big or small, there is a temptation to try to get through things on your own. Families often try to pull together and handle things in private. Individuals put up walls to protect their privacy, not wanting to appear "weak" or "needy."

But the fact is, we all need help from time to time, and

learning how to say "yes" is a huge step toward handling issues in a healthy manner.

When Betsy was first diagnosed, I initially assumed we would pull together, hunker down, and plow through the challenges. Then, as I realized what we were really going to be facing, I started to tell people, "yes."

- Yes, it would be great if you could organize meal deliveries.
- Sure, it would mean a lot if you would include Betsy in your prayer circle.
- We could really use help getting our yard in order. The weeds are out of control.
- I love the idea of a handprint quilt and think it would mean a lot to Betsy, Julia, and Molly. That would be amazing.

I came to realize that our friends and family were feeling as helpless as I was through much of this process. They wanted to do something—anything—to feel like they were making a difference. Saying "yes" not only eased the stress on our lives, it also allowed people to direct their own stress and concern into something positive.

Your problems don't have to be large to accept help. You just have to take a leap of faith and let people in.

Another way we opened ourselves up for help was by keeping people informed and letting them share in our journey and our struggles.

In most of my updates, I gave specific "call to action" bullet points that changed based on whatever Betsy was facing at the time, such as:

- Focus on Betsy's blood counts so she stays in remission.
- Help guide Betsy's new stem cells to her

bones, where they can set up shop and start producing blood cells.

- Focus on Betsy's lungs, helping eliminate the infections so she can be healthy enough to go home.

I realized that the hundreds of people who were following Betsy's story were her "team." It was our responsibility to give them instructions, to leverage their strength and energy toward the achievement of our goals.

I have had many people thank me for giving out "marching orders" in the updates. And I honestly felt like whenever I sent out a new message, Betsy and I could feel renewed energy and strength.

6. Pause to remember what is *really* important. There were times in the middle of Betsy's fight when I would think about our life before cancer. I would remember the problems that I thought I had, or the things that once "stressed me out." I would think about our past arguments or disagreements, and I would shake my head in disbelief. How could I have let those little things get to me?

The funny thing is, the little things still get to me from time to time. Betsy and I still have disagreements, like any couple. We get stressed about trivial things. Our priorities sometimes get out of whack.

Cancer doesn't eliminate misunderstandings or prevent us from getting irritable. But there are times when I stop, reflect, and remind myself of what is really important. My family, our friends, our health—these are the nonnegotiables in terms of priorities. Getting upset about dirty dishes is a luxury that in a strange way we are happy to have a chance to indulge.

When I get into bed at night, I often put my hand

on Betsy's forehead, just like I used to do every night when she was sick. Back then I was checking for a fever and saying a short prayer for her health. Now I do it as a reminder, as a connection to how far we've come and how lucky I really am.

I was lucky before the cancer. I'm lucky now. I sometimes need to pause long enough to remember that.

After all we've experienced, I don't believe cancer is a gift that Betsy and I received. If I could erase the word "leukemia" from the story of our lives together, I would do it in a second. Cancer is a part of who we are now, but I won't give it credit for what we do with the rest of our lives.

After all, it's not about the cancer.

About the Author

Brian Lucas lives in Minneapolis with his wife, Betsy, his daughters, Julia and Molly, and their dog, Bella.

Brian has spent decades telling stories. As an undergraduate at Princeton University, he worked on the nationally syndicated radio show *American Focus*, interviewing influential figures such as Tom Brokaw, Peter Jennings, Connie Chung, and Norman Mailer.

After college Brian pursued a career in journalism, interning with CNN in Washington, DC, then working as a reporter for Minnesota Public Radio. He earned a masters degree in Broadcasting from Northwestern University and began reporting for the CBS station in La Crosse, Wisconsin. After four years on the air, he returned to his hometown of Minneapolis to pursue a career in public relations. That's when he met Betsy, on a blind date.

Brian's PR career has taken him to Best Buy, Children's Hospitals and Clinics of Minnesota, and the University of Minnesota, where he is senior director of communications for the Academic Health Center.

Brian is chair of the Minnesota Chapter of the Leukemia Lymphoma Society board. In 2006, he was named to the *Twin Cities Business Journal*'s annual "40 Under 40" list of influential local business community members. He is a graduate of the Leadership Twin Cities program and completed the Policy Fellows program at the University of Minnesota Humphrey School of Public Affairs.